This book is one of a series of studies of Jewish community organization prepared by the Center for Jewish Community Studies of the Jerusalem Center for Public Affairs. English language studies in the series to date include:

The Balkan Jewish Communities: Yugoslavia, Bulgaria, Greece, and Turkey
>by Daniel J. Elazar, Harriet Pass Friedenreich, Baruch Hazzan, and Adina Weiss Liberles (1983)

Community and Polity: The Organizational Dynamics of American Jewry
>by Daniel J. Elazar (Jewish Publication Society, 1976)

The French Jewish Community by Ilan Greilsammer
>(forthcoming)

The Governance of Canadian Jewry edited by Harold M. Waller and Daniel J. Elazar (1983)

Jewish Communities in Frontier Societies: Argentina, Australia, South Africa
>by Daniel J. Elazar with Peter Y. Medding (Holmes and Meier, 1983)

The Jewish Communities of Scandinavia: Sweden, Denmark, Norway, and Finland
>by Daniel J. Elazar, Adina Weiss Liberles, and Simcha Werner (1983)

THE
BALKAN JEWISH
COMMUNITIES

YUGOSLAVIA, BULGARIA, GREECE AND TURKEY

Daniel J. Elazar,
Harriet Pass Friedenreich,
Baruch Hazzan, and
Adina Weiss Liberles

UNIVERSITY
PRESS OF
AMERICA

Center for Jewish Community
Studies of the Jerusalem
Center for Public Affairs

LANHAM • NEW YORK • LONDON

University Press of America,™ Inc.

4720 Boston Way
Lanham, MD 20706

3 Henrietta Street
London WC2E 8LU England

ISBN (Perfect): 0-8191-3474-0
ISBN   (Cloth): 0-8191-3473-2

All University Press of America books are produced on acid-free
paper which exceeds the minimum standards set by the National
Historical Publications and Records Commission.

This volume is dedicated to the Elazar and Abulafia families who were part and parcel of the communities described in the following pages for nearly 500 years, from the time of their exile from Spain until the Holocaust and mass <u>aliyah</u> to the reconstituted State of Israel.

PREFACE

This volume is a product of the worldwide study of Jewish community organization conducted since 1968 and under the auspices of the Center for Jewish Community Studies since its founding as the Jewish Community Studies Group in 1970. The Center for Jewish Community Studies is a research and educational institute devoted to the study of the organized Jewish community, past and present, and to the dissemination of its finding through teaching and publication, with a view toward enhancing the knowledge base used in making public policy decisions within Jewish life. The Center is built around a group of Fellows and Associates drawn from academic institutions in Israel and throughout the world and maintains offices in Jerusalem, Philadelphia, and Montreal. Since 1976, it has operated within the framework of the Jerusalem Center for Public Affairs.

The Study of Jewish Community Organization, one of the Center's principal projects, is a worldwide study of the dynamics of governance of all the organized countrywide Jewish communities presently in existence as they have been reconstituted since World War II. The initial effort within its framework was the "mapping" of the structures and functions of the organized Jewish communities in the world, a task never before undertaken. The studies in this volume were prepared in the mid-1970s as part of that effort. Except for the chapter on Greece, which was updated after that country returned to democratic rule, they reflect the situation at the end of the post war generation. As planned, they are in the nature of community maps which focus on communal structures and functions rather than full-fledged studies. The latter we have saved for the second stage of the research.

Funding for these studies was provided by a number of outside sources, as well as the Center for Jewish Community Studies. The Institute for Jewish Affairs of the World Jewish Congress and the Center for the Study of Federalism at Temple University provided initial support. Bar-Ilan University provided some support for the preparation of the chapter on Bulgaria. The revision of the chapter on Greece was funded by <u>Misgav Yerushalayim</u>, the Institute for the Study of the Sephardic and Oriental Heritage of the Hebrew University. The authors are most grateful to those agencies for their support.

The authors would also like to extend their thanks to the staff of the Jerusalem Center for Public Affairs for their assistance in bringing this volume to print. Special thanks are due Hannah Klieger and Hollis Dorman of the Philadelphia office and Judy Cohen in Jerusalem; Sarah Lederhendler and Linda Shor for their typing of manuscripts through their various versions; and Amy L. Lederhendler for editorial direction in Jerusalem.

DJE

Jerusalem

Kislev 5743 - December 1982

CONTENTS

LIST OF TABLES

GLOSSARY OF HEBREW TERMS

aliyah--literally means ascent or the act of going up; refers to the immigration of Jews to Israel

bet din--a Jewish religious court

hachsharah--a preparatory period before settlement in Israel

haftarah (pl. haftarot)--a prophetic selection read during the religious service on the Sabbath and festivals

halacha--Jewish oral and written law

halutz (pl. halutzim)--literally means a pioneer, usually refers to early Jewish settlers in Palestine

heder--elementary school for Jewish religious instruction

kashrut--Jewish dietary laws

kehilla (pl. kehillot)--distinctive Jewish form of local organization and government

kibbutz--a collective settlement in Israel

Lubavitch--hasidic community of worldwide scope whose original seat was in the Russian town of Lubavich

mikvah--a ritual Jewish bath

shaliach (pl. shlichim)--emissary

shechita--Jewish ritual slaughter of animals

shochet (pl. **shochatim**)--an officially licensed slaughterer of animals and poultry according to Jewish law

Talmud Torah--traditional Jewish school

yeshiva--a school for higher religious studies

THE SUNSET OF BALKAN JEWRY
Daniel J. Elazar

No region of Europe has a longer history of organized Jewish life than the Balkan Peninsula and the states located within it. The first diaspora communities outside of the Fertile Crescent were probably located in that region and Jewish settlement there has been continuous at least since the days of the Second Temple. During those long centuries, Jewish communal life has had its good periods and bad and has undergone several transformations. It has survived under Hellenistic, Roman, Byzantine, and Ottoman rule, and most recently, has been subjected to the rule of new states reflecting local national majorities.

The Jewish communities of the Balkan Peninsula have, themselves, passed into the hands of different segments of the Jewish people as the tides of war, economic and political change, and migration have crossed them. The seat of the first great European diaspora, the Balkan Jewish communities hosted the great conflict between Judaism and emergent Christianity. Throughout the Roman and Byzantine periods, the Balkans were under common imperial suzerainty and, as a result, their Jewish communities took on common characteristics. At the same time, years of isolation led to the development of a Jewish life separate in many ways from the mainstream of Jewish history, with separate rituals and customs, if not communal institutions. Isolated examples of that Roman or Greek Jewish pattern survived in small mountain communities until World War II.

The last great tide of Jewish migration into the Balkans came from the Iberian Peninsula beginning in the fifteenth century. Capitalizing on a combination of circumstances, the Sephardim brought the Balkans into the mainstream of Jewish life as they had not been for more than a millenium. By their sheer numbers, the Sephardim overwhelmed the indigenous Jewish communities, and, in effect, forced the latter to assimilate into the Judeo-Hispanic cultural and social framework which they brought with them. Ladino emerged to become the Jewish language of the Balkans in the way that Yiddish emerged to become the Jewish language of Eastern Europe. Moreover, exile from their beloved second motherland seemed to release great pent-up energies among the Sephardim which found their outlet in the Balkan setting.

The result was, at the very least, a silver age of Jewish culture bearing a distinctive Sephardic imprint whose impact shaped the entire Jewish world for two centuries. The cities of the Balkans, with Salonika heading the list, became bastions of Jewish life and culture. Sephardic halachic and kabbalistic creativity nourished in the region shaped Jewish life and thought from Russia to Latin America. It led, in time, to the last and greatest theo-political movement of pre-modern Jewry, the messianic movement of Sabbatai Zvi, a product of the Balkan Sephardic world.

Even after the region's decline and the passing of its hegemony over world Jewry to Eastern Europe, Balkan Jewry continued to enrich Jewish life and add to the store of Jewish learning. Sages, teachers and statesmen continued to emerge from its ranks and to make their impact, at least locally. Still at this late date, many great works of Balkan Jewish scholarship remain to be rediscovered and no adequate history of its Sephardic age has been written.

Balkan Jewry's age of greatness was first enhanced and then diminished by its location within the Ottoman Empire. The fall of Constantinople to the Ottoman forces in 1453 and the resulting consolidation of

2

Ottoman rule throughout the region, nearly forty years before the Spanish exile, provided Sephardic Jewry with a place of refuge that gave them sufficient scope for the exercise of their considerable talents. The Sephardim entered into a virtual alliance with the Imperial authorities to cooperate against the common Christian foe externally and to build a strong society internally. Their communities were given protected status within the framework of the Empire and their own power within existing communities was enhanced because of their relationship with the imperial authorities.

Balkan Jewry attained its highest development during the century that the Turks stood at the gates of Vienna. With the decline of the Empire, the Jewries within its borders also declined to some degree. In fact, the degree of their decline has been exaggerated because, with the passing of the major centers of Jewish life to other regions, general historians of the Jewish people neglected the Balkans. Jewish life continued to thrive and Jewish learning was still cultivated in the great Jewish cities.

In the nineteenth century, Balkan Jewry underwent something of a renaissance that was, unfortunately, cut short by the emergence of new nation-states out of the ruins of the Ottomans' European empire. The renaissance in its early stages featured the emergence of Ladino as a literary and intellectual medium that paralleled that of Yiddish in the lands to the north. It emphasized the modernization of Jewish education and, increasingly, a new political consciousness among Jews--whether in connection with local nationalism or Zionism. The Balkan haskalah (for the renaissance was part of that universal Jewish movement) gave rise to a modern literature, over 250 newspapers and journals, a systematization of Ladino grammar, and the like.

3

Economically, the condition of the urban communities of the Balkans also improved. The improvement was accompanied by substantial population growth through natural increase and, especially in the cities, through rural-urban migration. Finally, a series of constitutional and administrative reforms within the empire led to the restructuring of Jewish communal organization locally and the creation of a central authority for all Jews in the empire in Constantinople. While the western principle of individual citizenship was still only a glimmer for the future, the Jewish and other non-Muslim minorities were made increasingly equal in status with the empire's Muslim subjects over the course of the nineteenth century.

Before the Balkan wars and revolutions, this juridical change had little practical impact on the life of the community. The life of the community was drastically changed by the nationalistic revolutions that tore the empire apart in the years before World War I. A Jewish world that had been of one piece for at least 400 years, whose every linkage was based on the peace of the empire and whose every division cut across the new dividing lines established by the new nation-states, was suddenly put in a position of reorganizing its fragments from the ground up. The breakup of the host empire had far more impact on Balkan Jewry than did the breakup of the Czarist empire on Eastern European Jewry. Constantinople and Salonika, the empire's principal cities, were also its principal Jewish communities, unlike Moscow and Leningrad which were peripheral to Jewish life. Their separation from each other and from the other Balkan countries left many smaller communities cut off from their spiritual and cultural centers.

The Jewish communities in the new states had not been linked together with one another in any real way because they were all parts of the same imperial

4

polity. Now they had to forge such links. In doing so, they also modernized their community structures, borrowing from the experience of the nation-states of central Europe that had undergone a similar reorganization two to three generations earlier. Thus some version of the French consistoire or the German Kultusgemeinde pattern was reproduced in all of the new Balkan states, although frequently its external forms masked the continuation of older patterns.

In many respects, the new Jewish communities achieved a level of organizational perfection which they had never before approached. But, as has often been the case in Jewish history, organizational perfection was no indication of communal health. Indeed, quite the contrary is often the case, as was true of Balkan Jewry. Successful reorganization came simultaneously with the beginning of extensive assimilation and widespread loss of interest in things Jewish. Pressures from the host nations and the arrival of modernity began to take their toll. In some cases, Zionism provided a modern means of resuscitating communal vitality previously based on a common religious faith and culture but, in others, organized Zionism itself was harassed by the host state as inimical to the interests of its new-founded nationalism and could not become an operative force on the community.

World War I only intensified the new states' opposition to anything that smacked of Jewish separatism. The last vestiges of the Ottoman Empire were swept away and the modern Turkish state rose in its stead, to display the same kind of nationalism (in some respects even more xenophobic) that had previously emerged in the Balkan heartland. The Jews themselves were ambivalent regarding their own status. On the one hand, they welcomed their new rights to citizenship as individuals and began to assimilate into the larger society in most ways while, on the

5

other, they wished to preserve elements of the Jewish life they had known. During the 1920's and 1930's, they tried to create new ways to combine both, often in the face of considerable adversity.

Regardless of local conditions, for most of them World War II mooted the question. The Jewries of Greece and Yugoslavia were destroyed in the Holocaust. Bulgarian Jewry survived only to be engulfed in a Communist takeover leading them to migrate en masse to Israel. While Turkish Jewry was least physically un-affected by the war, the government's wartime economic measures brought severe hardship to most Jews and stimulated a mass migration once the Jewish state was established. Thus the once-powerful Jewries of the Balkans were reduced to mere shadows of their former selves, while their survivors were reunited within what had once been another corner of the Ottoman Empire and was now the center of the new Jewish renaissance.

In fact, the dissolution of Balkan Jewry began before the Holocaust. As in the case of Eastern European Jewry, the upheavals of the late nineteenth century generated a substantial out-migration of Jews from the region. Tens of thousands emigrated to the Western Hemisphere, settling in both North and Southern America. Other thousands moved to the Land of Israel before the establishment of the state to take part in its rebuilding. At the turn of the century, the four communities together contained over one third of a million Jews--more than the Jewish population of Canada today. Today, no more than 50,000 remain--a number equal to the Jewish population of Pittsburgh or the Tel Aviv suburb of Givatayim.

But Jewish communities do not disappear so easily. Thus in the years between 1949 and the present, those Jews who remained in the Balkan lands sought to rebuild their communities on a new and much smaller scale. The four studies in this volume document the political and organizational dimensions of their efforts in Bulgaria, Greece, Turkey and Yugoslavia. Under conditions where religious belief and practice have become minimal and even the most committed Jews had assimilated linguistically and culturally, those two dimensions have become more central to Jewish survival than ever before. In this respect the Balkan communities are simply at the extreme end of a continuum that includes most of the world's Jewries.

In all four countries, examined in the following pages, organizational and associational ties have come to occupy a disproportionate place in the life of the community, paralleled only by the persistence (albeit in a diminished way due to intermarriage) of family ties outside of the sphere of communal life. Jewish religion and culture count for relatively little but, in keeping with the modern temper, the tribal urge for group survival has taken on an associational character. It is an open question as to whether that format is sufficient to assure the survival that is sought; the evidence at this point is not very encouraging.

All four communities must make their way in countries dominated by regimes more or less antagonistic to the very notion of pluralism for non-territorial groups. Yugoslavia, the most liberal of the four because of its own character as a multi-national society with no single nation in the majority, has given the Jewish community the most room to maneuver by at least tacitly recognizing it as a semi-autonomous nationality albeit without an indigenous territorial base. But the complexities of Jewishness, involving a religious dimension and ties that cross political boundaries, not to speak of the complexities of Jews who do not want to separate themselves from the host society even as they wish to preserve some form of Jewish identity, generate their own limitations on the life of that community. From the perspective of the Yugoslav authorities, the Jewish community need not worry about its future; consequently, it may be the first to totally assimilate.

Bulgaria, on the other hand, is a textbook example of a Communist regime. Totalitarian to the core, its drive for internal homogeneity is reinforced by the existence of a clearly dominant national majority. No strong non-Bulgar minority exists and Jewish community life is further hampered by the intensely anti-religious aspects of Bulgarian Communism. On the other hand, the Bulgarians have proved to be relatively tolerant toward "their" Jews. Significantly, the community survives as an organized entity because of the authorities' felt need to use an ostensibly Jewish voice to denigrate Israel in the eyes of the surviving Jews.

Greece and Turkey are dominated by right-of-center, intensely nationalistic regimes. Greece, which has been under military domination since a 1967 coup, is governed by a classic right wing dictatorship. While its "colonels" have not been hostile to the Jewish community in any way, their generally nationalistic and authoritarian orientation has certainly made the Jewish communal leadership even more cautious than it was before 1967.

Turkey's regime has been more stable than that of Greece and the military plays a less direct role in the government. At the same time, Turkish nationalism is far more exclusive. Hence the advantages that

8

stability brings for the greater tolerance of internal differences are undercut by the continuing suspicion of "foreign" elements within Turkish society. Still, Turkish Jews are a known quantity to their hosts so the Turkish Jewish community can exist on two levels; a recognized outer religious framework protects an informally tolerated communal life of some variety.

All in all, organized Jewish life in the Balkan countries survives by careful consideration of local limitations on the part of each community's leadership. The same Jews are a nationality in Yugoslavia, strictly a religious group in Greece and Turkey, and no more than a Communist cultural association in Bulgaria. What is clear is that the four communities cannot undertake common action of the kind that could mobilize the resources of all 50,000 of their members, most of whom share a common heritage, to serve common purposes, in the place of the four fragments that exist today. Their host regimes are too hostile to one another to allow that. Indeed, the hostile cross currents separating them are "Balkan," if not "Byzantine," in their complexity.

III

In the end, each of the communities must depend upon outside assistance to enable it to survive. At least eight multi-country Jewish organizations have made their presence felt in one or more of the four communities in the twentieth century. The Alliance Israelite Universelle was the first. Its schools played a major role in the modernization of Balkan Jewry at the end of the nineteenth century. Education, however, became a most sensitive issue in states experiencing a wave of nationalistic sentiment and the Alliance was forced to withdraw from the

9

field. Indeed, even locally-sponsored Jewish schools have had their difficulties, where they have not been forced to close altogether.

The B'nai Brith was the next outside group to appear in the Balkans, where it became a meeting place for local Jewish elites. As the most prestigious symbol of modern association, B'nai Brith lodges easily became the places where the decisions shaping local communal life were taken. While most of the lodges have since disbanded, at least partly because of government opposition to their links with a foreign organization, in a few cases, they were transformed into independent local clubs and have continued to play important roles in local Jewish life.

While Zionism is generally thought to be an Ashkenazic movement, in fact, legally or otherwise, the World Zionist Organization became an important presence in all of the Balkan states very early in its history. Zionist societies antedate the first Zionist Congress (1897) and migration to Israel for purposes of rebuilding the land has been a fact of Balkan life for generations, if not centuries. The Bulgarian Jewish community was the first in the world to be dominated by organized Zionism. It is no exaggeration to say that no countrywide Jewish community was ever more thoroughly Zionist in orientation and politics than Bulgaria. Zionism has since become suspect or worse in all of the countries under consideration here, for reasons which should be obvious, given their nationalistic stances. As a consequence, organized Zionism was formally eliminated from every one of them.

The World Jewish Congress (WJC) and its predecessors once had an important role to play in securing and protecting the civil rights of Jews throughout the Balkans. While the WJC's effectiveness--never very great--has probably been diminished further in the aftermath of World War II, it remains the point of contact between world Jewry and the various Balkan communities most likely to be tolerated by the current regimes. Even so, formal links are discouraged or forbidden in three of the four countries.

The distributive organizations of world Jewry have all played some role in the Balkans. The Joint Distribution Committee, the Claims Conference, and the Memorial Foundation for Jewish Culture all played a significant role in the reconstruction of those communities laid low by World War II. As sources of funds and, in some cases, technical expertise, they are substantially responsible for whatever exists today in the way of Jewish services in the Balkans, at least outside of Turkey.

In recent years, Israel has assumed a central--if usually unofficial--role in the maintenance of Jewish life in the Balkans. The story of its activities cannot yet be told. Suffice it to say that its impact on Balkan Jewry is a textbook example for those who argue on behalf of Israel's centrality in Jewish life. If the Balkan Jewish communities do survive as active entities and even participate in contemporary Jewish life, it will be in no small measure because of Israel's existence and active efforts on their behalf.

THE JEWISH COMMUNITY OF YUGOSLAVIA
Harriet Pass Friedenreich

Less than 7,000 Jews now live in Yugoslavia and fewer than 6,000 individuals are formally affiliated with the Jewish community. Of the thirty-six organized Jewish communities within the country, the three largest and most important are located in Belgrade, Zagreb and Sarajevo. Some Jewish communal activity is to be found in eight other cities, namely, Subotica, Novi Sad, Osijek, Rijeka, Zemun, Split, Ljubljana and Skoplje, but for the most part, the remaining twenty-five Jewish communities exist primarily on paper, since they do not have enough members to support any kind of real communal life. Several of these "communities" have less than ten members apiece, while a few hundred Jews live in places where there is no formal community whatsoever. Jewish communal activity in Yugoslavia is concentrated almost exclusively in those localities with a Jewish population of over 100, while the major centers are those with over 1,000 members each.[1]

Although there are traces of Jewish settlement in Dalmatia and Macedonia which date back as far as Roman times and also in Slovenia and Serbia in the Middle Ages, the first major wave of Jewish immigration to the South Slav lands came after the expulsion of the Jews from Spain in 1492. By the mid-sixteenth century, Sephardic settlers had ventured into the interior of the Ottoman Empire, establishing communities in such towns as Skoplje (Üsküb) and Bitolj (Monastir) in Macedonia, Belgrade in Serbia and Sarajevo in Bosnia. Sephardic communities also grew up in Dubrovnik (Ragusa) and Split (Spalato) on the Dalmatia coast. These communities remained fairly small, with some further immigration from Italy and other parts of the Ottoman Empire, but in the late nineteenth century, they received considerable numbers

12

of newcomers from Bulgaria and the rest of the Balkans. The Sephardim thus lived almost exclusively in the former Ottoman territories, including Serbia, Bosnia, and Macedonia, as well as in Dalmatia.

By contrast, the Ashkenazic communities in the former Habsburg areas were all of fairly recent origin. Until the late eighteenth century, Jews had been banned from residence in Slovenia, Croatia and the Military Frontier (except for the town of Zemun or Semlin across the Danube from Belgrade). During the nineteenth and early twentieth centuries, a large number of Jews from various parts of the Austro-Hungarian Empire migrated to the South Slav regions under Hungarian control. Major Jewish communities developed in Zagreb (Agram, Zagrab) and Osijek (Essig, Eszek) in Croatia-Slavonia and Novi Sad (Neusatz, Ujvidek) and Subotica (Szabadka) in the Vojvodina, while there were many other small towns in these districts with significant Jewish populations as well.

After the occupation of Bosnia-Hercegovina by Austria-Hungary in 1878, some Ashkenazic Jews moved to Bosnia, especially its capital, Sarajevo. The Ashkenazic community in Belgrade also grew up around the same time. Conversely, a small Sephardic settlement eventually appeared in Zagreb. On the whole, however, the line of demarcation between the Ashkenazim and the Sephardim continued to follow the old border between Habsburgs and Ottomans.

Following the creation of the Yugoslav state in 1918, the Ashkenazim comprised two-thirds of the Jewish population and the Sephardim, the remaining third. The two groups formed separate communities, even when they lived in the same locality, as, for example, in the three major centers of Belgrade, Zagreb and Sarajevo. A small group of Orthodox Jews, mainly centered in the Vojvodina, also established their own recognized communities. In 1930, 114

13

organized Jewish communities existed in Yugoslavia: thirty-eight were Sephardic, seventy Ashkenazic-Neologue and six Ashkenazic-Orthodox.[2] The Sephardic and Ashkenazic-Neologue comunities together constituted a Federation of Jewish Religious communities of Yugoslavia, whereas the Orthodox communities set up their own Union of Orthodox Jewish Religious Communities.

On the eve of World War II, the Jewish population in Yugoslavia was estimated to total 71,342, of whom 68,710 were Yugoslav citizens and 2,632 foreign nationals.[3] The Holocaust destroyed over three-quarters of Yugoslav Jewry. In the different parts of the country, the various occupying forces, together with some local Fascists, systematically tried to exterminate the community. Some Jews managed to save themselves by joining the partisans or escaping to Italian-held territory.

In 1946, 12,414 Jews remained in Yugoslavia. About half of these were Sephardic and half Ashkenazic. Fifty-six Jewish communities were reconstituted, the largest of which were Belgrade (2,236), Zagreb (2,126) and Sarajevo (1,413).[4] The former distinctions between Ashkenazim and Sephardim, Neologue and Orthodox were no longer retained. Every local community included all the Jews in its vicinity and all communities belonged to one central federation.

Soon after the creation of the state of Israel, the Yugoslav authorities permitted Jews to emigrate there freely, if they so desired. At first, doctors and other professionals were discouraged from leaving, but later they too were allowed to go with their families. Non-Jewish spouses were also given permission to leave the country. Between 1948 and 1952, 7,578 persons departed for Israel in a series of five aliyot.[5] Thereafter, individuals could follow if and when they chose. About 150 Jews returned from Israel to Yugoslavia, while others made their way from there to North America, where there were already several existing small Yugoslav Jewish emigre colonies. After more than half the surviving population had gone on aliya to Israel, a Jewish community of 6,000, to 7,000 remained in Yugoslavia.

Since 1952, there has been very little migration by Jews either to or from Yugoslavia. The overall population of the Jewish community as a whole remained fairly constant until around 1970, when a decline began to occur. Within the country, there has been some internal movement of Jews from smaller to middle size or larger centers. In 1939, 71.9 percent of the Jewish population lived in the 10 largest centers. This figure had increased to 77 percent by 1946. By 1958, over 85 percent of Yugoslav Jewry was registered in the 10 largest communities. The size of the three major communities has not increased very greatly, however. Between 1952 and 1969, the Belgrade Jewish population grew from 1,380 to 1,602; Zagreb from 1,287 to 1,341 and Sarajevo from 1,028 to 1,090.[6] In general, it seems that relatively few people returned to their previous places of residence after the war or have remained permanently in the town where they were born.

The ratio between Sephardim and Ashkenazim in the overall Jewish population has remained relatively constant from the interwar period to the present. According to a 1971 demographic survey, about one-third of Yugoslav Jews had Sephardic parentage and about one-half, Ashkenazic parentage, while slightly less than five percent were of mixed Sephardic-Ashkenazic origin and the remaining 10 percent considered themselves to be Jews without futher specification.[7] The line of demarcation between them no longer exists to the extent which prevailed previously, however. Some Sephardim have crossed over

15

from the poorer and less developed areas of Macedonia, Bosnia and Serbia to the wealthier regions, such as Croatia or even Slovenia. No official distinctions are presently made between Ashkenazim and Sephardim and the differences between them are gradually disappearing, especially among the younger generation. Among the older people, particularly the small group with more traditional leanings, minor squabbles between the two elements have not vanished completely. All communal institutions and organizations are unified, however, and social ties undoubtedly exist as well.

In 1971, at the time of the latest Yugoslav general census, a survey of Yugoslav Jewry was conducted by the Federation of Jewish Communities of Yugoslavia. Out of some 5,696 registered members, 4,702 individuals (or 85 percent) were interviewed and detailed questionnaires were completed. In Belgrade, 1,010 members of the community (or 63 percent) cooperated; in Zagreb, 1,122 (or 84 percent) were contacted (of whom 102 lived in the Jewish Home for the Aged, 959 resided elsewhere in Zagreb proper and the rest in outlying towns); in Sarajevo, 825 (or 76 percent) participated.[8] These replies provide a reasonably accurate picture of the structure of these communities, the age and origin of their membership and their economic distribution. They also cast considerable light on the extent of communal activity, as well as the incidence of intermarriage.

According to this study, in each of the three major communities, well over half the membership was over 45 years of age: in Belgrade, 58.3 percent; in Zagreb, 70.3 percent; and in Sarajevo, 52.8 percent. Less than ten percent were found to be under 15: 6.1 percent in Belgrade, 5.4 percent in Zagreb and 8.8 percent in Sarajevo. The Jewish community, then, is by and large an "old" one, with fewer and fewer children available to fill the ranks in the future.

16

These communities are composed very heavily of natives of Yugoslavia. Eighty percent of the Jews in Belgrade and Zagreb claimed Serbo-Croatian as their mother tongue, while 92.9 percent did so in Sarajevo. Roughly one-third of the members of the Belgrade and Zagreb communities were born in the city in which they now reside, while almost 60 percent of those living in Sarajevo spent their earliest years there as well. For reasons which are not entirely clear, Sarajevo seems to have a younger and more indigenous Jewish population than the two larger centers.

The economic condition of the Jewish population is, in general, fairly good, especially according to Yugoslav standards. The community gives intermittent monetary aid to several hundred needy persons, usually to those elderly or sick who cannot support themselves, but poverty is not a major problem among Jews. Their economic well-being would seem to be quite uniform in the various parts of the country, unlike the situation before World War II when there were much greater discrepancies between different regions.

In the interwar period, most Jews were involved in business, crafts and private white collar jobs, while some were engaged in the free professions as well. Under the Communist regime, the economic structure of the country has changed drastically and the Jews have been obliged to adapt themselves to the new circumstances or else leave. As a result, the Jews remaining in Yugoslavia tended to be mainly professionals or civil servants, many holding high positions in these fields. This rather peculiar occupational distribution may be partially accounted for, on the one hand, by the survival of a high percentage of the Jewish professional class who were reserve officers in the Royal Yugoslav Army and hence became German military prisoners-of-war during World War II, and, on the other hand, the policy of the authorities to discourage the emigration of these professionals, especially medical doctors.

Table 2-1 provides a comparison of the occupational structure of Yugoslav Jewry in 1953 and 1971. It is clear that a high proportion of the Jewish population is engaged in professional occupations. According to the 1971 demographic study, in Belgrade, out of 333 persons gainfully employed, 141 (or 42.4 percent) may be so classified; in Zagreb, out of 328, 161 or (47.9 percent) fall into this category; and in Sarajevo, 157 out of 288 (55.9 percent) may also be considered professionals. Consequently, the number of persons with higher education is quite impressive-- roughly one-third of the survey respondents in Belgrade and Zagreb and close to a quarter in Sarajevo. In economic terms, at least, the Jews would seem to belong to an elite group within Yugoslav urban society.

The Jewish community considers as Jewish virtually anyone who wishes to be considered as such. Certainly, one Jewish parent is sufficient criterion for an individual to be accepted as a "member in good standing" of the community. Non-Jewish spouses are also eligible for membership. The key to this lenient policy of acceptance within the community lies in the extremely high rate of intermarriage in Yugoslavia. Of 4,702 communal members responding to the 1971 demographic survey, 3,209 persons, or 68 percent, had two Jewish parents, 1,028 individuals, or 22 percent, had one Jewish parent, and 465 registered members, or 10 percent, reported neither parent to have been Jewish. In the 2,557 households of respondents, 4,199 people out of a possible 6,457, or 65 percent, declared themselves to be Jews. Significantly, of the 102 residents of the Jewish Home for the Aged in Zagreb, 95 reported both parents Jewish and none had only one Jewish parent, while seven had no Jewish parentage. The older generation, then, are rarely, if

18

Table 2-1

Occupational Distribution of Yugoslav Jewry

Occupations	1953[a] Total	%	1971[b] Total	%
White collar workers[c]	875	37.1	363	22.9
Craftsmen and industrial workers[d]	277	11.7	230	14.5
Commercial Employees[e]	247	10.5	92	5.8
Physicians, pharmacists and other health workers	262	11.1	203	12.8
Professors, teachers and other instructors	102	4.3	183	11.5
Lawyers and economists[f]	72	3.0	113	7.1
Construction engineers, architects, etc.	82	3.5	59	3.7
Physicists, chemists, mathematicians, etc.[g]			91	5.7
Biologists, agronomists, veterinarians, etc.	25	1.1	21	1.3
Managerial personnel[g]			62	3.9
Army officers[h]	78	3.3		
Journalists and media personnel	31	1.3	34	2.2
Artists and writers	33	1.4	43	2.7
Other	277	11.7	93	5.9
TOTAL	2,361	100.0	1,587	100.0

(a) Source: Dr. Albert Vajs, "Jevreji u novoj Jugoslaviji," Jevrejski Almanah (N.S.), 1954, p. 36; Institute of Jewish Affairs of the World Jewish Congress, European Jewry Ten Years after the War (New York, 1956), pp. 190-191; (b) Source: Marko Peric, "Demographic Study of the Jewish Community in Yugoslavia, 1971-72," Papers in Jewish Demography 1973 (Jerusalem, 1973), p. 272; (c) In 1958 listed under "civil servants" and in 1971 listed under "financial, office and related employees"; (d) In 1953 listed separately as "artisans" and "factory technicians"; (e) In 1953 listed as "in economic fields"; (f) In 1953 included lawyers, judges and other legalists, but not economists; (g) Not listed as a separate category in 1953; (h) Not listed as a separate category in 1971.

ever, the products of mixed marriages and are less likely to have married outside of the community. Among the middle and younger generations, however, intermarriage seems to be the general rule rather than the exception. This phenomenon has been steadily on the increase since World War II. The community is small and scattered throughout the country; hence the likelihood for one young Jew to marry another is quite limited.

Conversion does not enter in as a factor in these intermarriages. Even if the non-Jewish partner were willing to convert, there is no one qualified to perform the conversion. By the same token, there are no Jewish weddings, and religious practices in general are played down. The Jewish partners to mixed marriages are fully accepted as members of the Jewish community and their non-Jewish spouses are accepted to a certain degree as well. Many persons involved in mixed marriages are fairly active in Jewish affairs and their children often participate extensively in Jewish activities. The Jewish community seems to have acknowledged that intermarriage is an inevitable feature of Jewish life in Yugoslavia and they try to make the best of it by retaining as many of their members as possible. This attitude has enabled the community to remain reasonably stable in its membership.

Relations between the Jewish community and Yugoslav society at large are generally cordial. There has never been a strong tradition of anti-Semitism in the country, although Nazi propaganda before and during World War II has left its mark. Anti-Semitic incidents, such as vandalism of Jewish cemeteries, occur only rarely and are, as a rule, vigorously opposed by the authorities. The Jewish community does not perceive local anti-Semitism as a major problem and a friendly atmosphere is usually maintained. The community takes pride in this sympathetic ambiance and the more specific manifestations of government support and strives to consolidate both.

The Jewish community and its leadership fully supported Tito and the Yugoslav brand of Communism. The top leadership often holds, or has held, high government positions as well and they are, for the most part, members of the League of Communists. In the early post-war years, the Jewish community even participated in national election campaigns in support of the government, presumably to display its loyalty to the regime. Government representatives regularly attend all major conferences, celebrations or commemorations held within the community. It is clearly very important for the community to foster these close official ties.

Non-Jews do not concern themselves to any great extent with Jewish communal life; however, individual non-Jews participate in Jewish activities. Thus non-Jewish children attend the Jewish kindergartens, non-Jewish students are to be found at Jewish student club meetings, and non-Jews take part in the Jewish choirs.

The general media seem to have adopted a double standard regarding Yugoslav Jews on the one hand and Israel on the other. What little is reported on Jews per se and Yugoslav Jews in particular is sympathetic and balanced, but the same cannot be said for reporting on the Middle East. Although Yugoslavia was one of the first countries to recognize the State of Israel in 1948, since then official policy has increasingly tended toward support for the Arab cause. The bias of the Yugoslav press against Israel is very pronounced; such a stand cannot help but influence the Jewish community and its behavior.

The Jewish community is obviously rather sensitive on this issue, since its spokesmen for the

21

most part continue to be openly pro-Israel, but there
is little that they can do about the situation. The
leadership, however, tends to be quite defensive if
any foreign source attacks the Yugoslav press as being
anti-Semitic. In 1969, the Federation of the Jewish
Communities sent a letter of rebuttal to the London
Jewish Chronicle which had published an article under
the headline "Yugoslav Papers Become Anti-Semitic."
They accused the Chronicle not only of being sensa-
tionalist but in addition of not serving the best
interests of Jewry in Yugoslavia or Jewry in general.
They concluded the letter by stating: "It is necessary to point out that the Yugoslav state and political organization have always taken a correct stand on
the national question in general and especially have
also maintained a correct relationship with the Jewish
community."[9]

Specialized Jewish sources and the foreign press
are far more important than the local Yugoslav media
in providing Yugoslav Jews with accurate information
on Jewish issues and shaping their self-perceptions.
The bi-monthly Jevrejski pregled (Jewish Review) which
is published by the Federation of Jewish Communities
contains news from Israel and the Jewish world at
large, as well as local current events and excerpts
from the Yugoslav press. The writer found that most
of the Jews whom she met in Yugoslavia, including many
Jewish students, were remarkably well-informed about
what was going on in Jewish life in Israel and in the
United States.

The Structure of the Yugoslav Jewish Community

The Jewish community of Yugoslavia is very
tightly organized both on the countrywide and local
levels. The Federation of Jewish Communities serves

as the "roof" organization for all the local communities. All Jewish organizations and institutions are subsidiary to the local community and in turn to the Federation, which coordinates all activities on a countrywide scale. No intermediate territorial bodies exist on the republic level.

The community as a whole is extremely unified structurally. Separate Sephardic and Ashkenazic communities no longer operate and no distinctions are made between members of the two groups in any organization or institution. This situation contrasts sharply with the state of affairs before the war, when within the countrywide federation separate Ashkenazic and Sephardic communities functioned on the local level, each with a wide variety of associated but independent charitable and cultural organizations. Since the war, the multiplicity of local bodies has been eliminated completely, in part due to expediency, considering the small size of the population, but also out of a desire for uniformity and cohesiveness.

The Federation of Jewish Communities with its member communities provides an all-embracing communal organization with no exceptions. Together they comprise the entire organized Jewish community and account for all of its activities. The Federation and the local communal administrations are thus by far the most important and powerful Jewish bodies in the country, since they control Jewish life entirely.

Religious institutions operate within the framework of the local communities but play a very secondary and limited role. Since the war, there has been no chief rabbinate and, indeed, since 1968, there have been no properly qualified rabbis in the country at all. Although synagogues still operate in the larger centers, the community is totally lay-controlled and almost completely secular in orientation.

23

Before World War II, membership within the Jewish community was compulsory by state law for all Jews living in Yugoslavia. Since the war, however, membership has become an entirely voluntary matter. Membership is open to all persons of Jewish descent who do not belong to any other religious community and who voluntarily state that they want to become members of the community. The spouse and children of such persons are also eligible for membership if they fulfill the same conditions. Persons who fall under neither of the above categories but wish to become members of the Jewish community may be admitted upon written request at the discretion of the communal leadership.[10]

One thus becomes a member of the community by formally stating that one wishes to do so. Any member can leave the community by submitting a written statement. Membership is generally an individual matter, although families of members of the community are also eligible to join. It often happens, however, that the individual who is of Jewish descent becomes a member of the community, while his or her non-Jewish spouse and their children do not. A person must belong to the Jewish community in the locality of his residence and he may not be a member of more than one community in the country.

It is possible to associate oneself with the community without formally becoming a member by belonging to one of its organizations, participating in certain of its activities or contributing towards its support. Such affiliation, e.g., belonging to one of the choirs, which might be preferred by some products of mixed marriages, for example, is not considered equivalent to being a registered member of the community since non-Jews may also join the choir and participate in similar Jewish communal activities if they so choose.

24

An accurate estimate of the total number of individuals eligible for membership in the Jewish community is not available. An indeterminate number of persons of Jewish descent do not acknowledge their Jewish connections and have no affiliation with the community whatsoever. It is assumed, however, that this group is relatively small. In 1965, 6,879 persons were registered as Jews, i.e., officially acknowledged their Jewish affiliation, while 6,197 persons were formally members of the Jewish community. Thus, 90 percent of the self-acknowledged Jews officially belonged to the community.[11] In 1974, updated communal records revealed a total of 5,696 registered members, an 8 percent decline since the previous decade.[12]

The number of Jews recorded in the Yugoslav census results is substantially lower than the actual membership within the Federation of Jewish Communities. The 1953 census was the only one in the postwar period which contained a question on religion, as well as one on nationality. In that year, 2,565 persons were enumerated as belonging to the "Mosaic faith," whereas 2,307 individuals declared themselves to be Jews by nationality. Interestingly, approximately half of the Jews by religion claimed to be part of some Slavic nationality (or else Hungarian), whereas almost half of those who considered themselves Jews by nationality did not identify themselves as Jews by religion. The 1961 census reported 2,110 Jews by nationality, approximately one-third of the total membership in the various Jewish communities. Ten years later, the census results showed a phenomenal increase, doubling the number of Jews by nationality to 4,811. According to a critical analysis of the date, however, much of this apparent jump was probably due to computer error.[13] In any event, there are clearly many more Jews living in Yugoslavia than appear in official government statistics.

In 1954, Dr. Albert Vajs, who was then president of the Federation of Jewish Communities, categorized the Jews remaining in Yugoslavia into five types: (a) those who considered themselves Jews by nationality but not members of any religious community; (b) those who considered themselves Jews by nationality and also members of the Jewish ("Mosaic") faith; (c) those who considered themselves as Jews by religion but Serbs or Croats by nationality; (d) persons of Jewish descent who considered themselves members of another nationality and who did not belong to any religious community, but still showed a certain interest in Jewish life and participated in some activities; and (e) Jews by descent who did not consider themselves Jews by religion or by nationality and who no longer maintained ties with Jewry or showed interest in the life of the community. Dr. Vajs pointed out that these variations were not always sharply defined and that individuals often switched back and forth from one category to another. For the community, however, the first two types, which represented the vast majority of the organized Jewish community in Yugoslavia, formed the most important element, while the third type also played a significant role.[14] Types (a), (b), and (c) thus constituted the members, type (d) the affiliates and type (e) the non-affiliates.

It is not completely clear exactly who does not affiliate today and why. Immediately after the war, many Jews who had been among the leading partisans and subsequently held high government or army positions chose not to affiliate with the community but rather to identify themselves entirely with the new state. Today, this attitude is no longer prevalent on any large scale, although individual examples undoubtedly can be found. Probably, most Jews who do not feel the need to affiliate adopt this position on personal rather than political grounds. They have become entirely indifferent to the community because they have intermarried and become part of non-Jewish society and, in the process, have lost contact with their past.

It would be perfectly possible for an individual to acknowledge his Jewish origins privately but not publicly. There is little way actually to manifest one's Jewishness without some minimal affiliation, however. It would seem to be rather difficult to successfully deny one's Jewishness completely. Conversion is no longer a feasible alternative in contemporary Yugoslavia. It is generally known who is a Jew, especially if both one's parents were Jews. There is, however, no particular stigma attached to a person of Jewish origin, hence there is no real necessity to deny one's background. It is this writer's impression, at least, that with very few exceptions, Yugoslav Jews do not feel the need to go out of their way to hide their Jewish descent.

The Jewish community of Yugoslavia is recognized as both a "national" and a "religious" community, although there are no longer any special laws which define its existence, such as the Law of the Religious Community of Jews in Yugoslavia of 1929. The community is allowed to conduct its religious affairs freely, according to the general laws on the legal position of religious communities in Yugoslavia which was passed in 1953 and the principle of freedom of religion and conscience as guaranteed in the constitution.

The Federation of Jewish Communities is recognized by the government as the representative of the Jewish population. Other Jewish organizations and institutions within the community acquire legal status through their association with the Federation. There are no outside Jewish bodies operating in Yugoslavia today.

The general courts have complete jurisdiction over Jewish affairs. There is no longer a functioning Bet Din, hence the communal authorities have little control over matters of Jewish status. Marriage and divorce are entirely under civil control; there does not appear to be any Jewish religious marriage or divorce in present-day Yugoslavia. The dietary laws are also not observed. The community itself is to a large extent responsible for the non-observance of these traditionally Jewish matters, not the state. An explanation for the existing situation can be found in th lack of qualified religious personnel on the one hand and on the strongly secularist attitude of the Jewish leadership on the other.

The Federation of Jewish Communities has had its own written constitution since 1956 and the communities are obliged to have their own constitutions as well. The first post-war constitution of the Federation was drawn up by a specially appointed committee within the Federation and adopted at the Seventh National Conference of Jewish Communities held in Belgrade in 1956. This constitution was revised several times and in 1970 a new constitution was introduced at the annual conference of the Federation.

The key to an understanding of the structure of the Jewish community in Yugoslavia lies in an exploration of the Federation of Jewish Communities and its development over the past sixty years. In 1919, the Federation of Jewish Religious Communities of Yugoslavia came into being. Its statutes were ratified by the government in 1921 and in 1929, its position was legally defined by the Law on the Religious Community of Jews in the Kingdom of Yugoslavia. The official role of the Federation was to act as the liaison between the government authorities and the local Jewish communities and among the Jewish communities themselves. The Federation represented the Jewish community to the outside world, administered government subsidies, and conducted defense activities on behalf of Yugoslav and foreign Jews. Together with the Chief Rabbinate and the Rabbinical Synod, it also supervised religious and educational affairs and settled religious and other disputes within the Jewish community at large. During the interwar period, the authority of the Federation over its member communities was extensive but never complete, since many other organizations and institutions, such as the Zionist Federation, the Sephardic Organization and B'nai Brith, functioned outside its sphere of influence. With the German occupation of Yugoslavia in April of 1941, the Federation was forced to cease its operations temporarily.

In October 1944, the Federation resumed its activities under its former president, Dr. Friedrich Pops. In the immediate postwar period, it occupied itself primarily with humanitarian tasks, such as taking care of the returnees from the concentration camps, the sick, the elderly and the orphaned. From 1945 to 1952, the Autonomous Committee for Aid, established in conjunction with the American Joint Distribution Committee, worked together with the Federation in assisting the Jewish community in its recovery. Another major task of the Federation in the late 'forties and early 'fifties was to help with the emigration to Israel.[15] It was only after 1952 that the Federation was able to consolidate its power and reorganize itself and its activities to correspond to the needs of those Jews who had remained in the country.

The Federation now serves as the coordinating body for all Jewish activities in the country. Its primary concern has shifted from religious to cultural concerns. In 1952, the Federation deleted the word "Religious" from its official title in order to indicate this change and to stress that it was concerned with all aspects of communal life, national, cultural, educational, etc. Within its framework, it includes coordinating committees for the women's sections, youth and choirs, numerous specialized commissions and councils (the Commission on Cultural Activities; the Commission for Work with Students; the Commission for Finance and Welfare; the Commission for General Business and the Council on Inter-Ethnic and International Relations), as well as representatives of the various institutions which it runs, such as the Home for the Aged in Zagreb, the Jewish Historical Museum in Belgrade, the annual summer camp and the Jewish press. The Federation is thus an all-embracing body which controls all matters relating to the community internally and externally.

The governing bodies of the Federation are the Conference of Communities, a Center Board (until 1970), and an Executive Board, which includes a Working Committee and the Presidency, along with a Supervisory Board and the sub-committees for specialized fields.[16] The Conference of Communities is considered the highest body within the Federation. It is composed of representatives of all communities with at least 15 registered members. The number of delegates per community is determined by size: communities with 15 to 100 members may send one delegate each; with 101 to 200, two delegates each; 201-1000 members, three delegates each and over 1000 members, five delegates each. The communities select their own delegates for the Conference, with the exception of the members of the Executive Board who are automatically delegated to the Conference and are included among the total to be sent from their community. The Conference is held annually and decides practical questions connected with the working policy of the community, such as the budget and so forth. Every three years it elects new members to the Executive Board and other bodies.

The Executive Board, which in 1970 was expanded so as to replace the Central Committee and represent all the large communities, has 26 members: 11 are elected by the Conference from among the Belgrade community, four are members by virtue of their office, i.e., the president of the communities of Belgrade, Zagreb and Sarajevo and the secretary of the Federation, and nine members are delegated by the nine largest communities; in addition, one member represents the Directory of the Home for the Aged in Zagreb. The Executive Board must meet at least every two months.

The Working Committee of the Federation, which consists of the Belgrade members of the Executive Board plus the vice-presidents of the Federation, takes care of the day-to-day business of the Federation and meets as often as is necessary. From its members and outside workers the various committees and sub-committees of the Executive Board are formed.

The Presidency consists of the president and substitute president (both of whom must be from Belgrade), the vice-presidents and the secretary. These officers are elected by the Conference of Communities and form part of the Executive Board and Working Committee.

Each local Jewish community encompasses all Jewish institutions and organizations within its locality. The community is run by a communal council, which is elected annually or biennially, according to the regulations of its statutes. Day-to-day administration is in the hands of an executive board composed of the president, vice-president, secretary and treasurer, plus the heads of the various sub-committees and sections. Among the subsidiary bodies are, for example in Belgrade, financial, cultural, social, property and legal committees, cemetery administration, plus religious, women's, youth and choir sections.[17]

In each of the larger communities, the most important organizations are generally the women's section, the youth section and the choir (in Belgrade and Zagreb). These are the most active, since they meet regularly and sponsor a variety of programs. The religious institutions occupy a secondary position in the community. In the larger centers, religious services are held regularly on Friday evenings and on holidays.

In theory, the structure of all the Yugoslav Jewish communities is uniform, but in the smaller localities it is rarely complete. Only the major communities are able to maintain a full array of communal activities. Thus, Belgrade, Zagreb and Sarajevo offer the most complete programs, while the six medium size communities (with from 100 to 500 members) operate on a smaller scale. The remaining tiny communities offer a bare minimum of communal activities.

The Jewish community in Yugoslavia is engaged primarily in cultural, educational, youth and social welfare activities and secondarily in religious affairs. Most activities are carried out on the local plane but some spheres are handled almost exclusively by the Federation, such as defense, general fund-raising and publications.

The community's chief interest is to ensure its own survival, hence it places great emphasis on youth and cultural development. Welfare work is also considered an on-going need. In its attempt to preserve its past heritage, the community concerns itself with its historical museum and archives, erecting monuments to those who died in the Holocaust

32

and looking after cemeteries. Of less importance is the religious aspect of communal life. Religious facilities are maintained primarily for the benefit of those of the older generation who still follow traditional Jewish patterns of observance to some degree.

The community tends to serve the young and the old but the so-called "middle generation" (between 25 and 45) is generally left out of its activities. The leadership perceives this as a major problem, but thus far has not managed to discover a solution to this dilemma. According to the 1971 survey, in Saravejo, 289 persons, or 38.4 percent of those over 15 years of age replying to the questionnaire, claimed to have participated in Jewish activities since World War II. This figure dropped to 213 individuals, or 22.7 percent of the respondents in Belgrade while in Zagreb, only 147 or 17 percent, indicated participation. It would appear that Sarajevo has the most vibrant community of the three; this impression was indeed borne out by the writer's personal experience there as well. On the whole, however, the level of participation in Jewish organizations is relatively low.

Cultural matters occupy a position of great important within the communal framework. In the larger centers, lectures, films and various other programs on Jewish topics are sponsored by the local community. The women's sections of the communities hold regular teas with speakers and discussions on subjects of Jewish interest. The youth groups, too, have cultural programs, talks and debates on current problems in the Jewish world.

The Belgrade and Zagreb Jewish communities each have their own Jewish choir. The choirs, Braca Baruh in Belgrade (named after three Jewish brothers who were active partisans in World War II) and Mose

33

Pijade in Zagreb (named after the foremost Jewish Communist leader in Yugoslavia), cultivate both Jewish and Yugoslav music, with songs in their repertoire in Hebrew, Yiddish, Ladino and Serbo-Croatian. They perform at Jewish functions, compete in Yugoslav music festivals, give their own concerts and have toured Europe and Israel several times. The membership in these choirs ranges in age from young to middle-aged. Some of the vocalists are non-Jews.

The larger Jewish communities have their own Jewish libraries and reading rooms, which contain books and newspapers of general Jewish interest in Serbo-Croatian and foreign languages (mainly German). The most extensive of these facilities is connected with the Federation in Belgrade, while the Zagreb Jewish community houses a fine private collection of Judaica from the interwar period which belongs to a former Zagreb Jewish lawyer, Dr. Lavoslav Schick.

The Federation also maintains the Jewish Historical Museum and Archive in Belgrade, which amasses and tastefully displays materials pertaining to the history of Yugoslav Jewry. (In Saravejo, there is a Jewish museum for Bosnia-Hercegovina which is run by the state.) In addition to documents and artifacts, an attempt is being made to record local Jewish folklore, especially Ladino songs and music.

The Federation has encouraged scholarly research and literary productivity in the Jewish field by offering annual awards for works pertaining to the Yugoslav Jewish experience. Between 1955 and 1969, 462 entries were submitted for this competition, of which 147 won prizes, thirty-seven for scholarly research, 106 for literature and four for musical compositions.[18] Most of the literary works submitted have tended to deal with the Holocaust. Both Jews and non-Jews have competed for these monetary awards and many of these works have been published in Jevrejski

34

almanah. The Memorial Foundation for Jewish Culture also offers scholarships to individual Yugoslav Jews interested in studying some aspect of Judaica abroad.

The Yugoslav Jewish community publishes a bi-monthly called Jevrejski pregled (Jewish Review) in some 3,500 copies, which is sent to every registered Jewish household in the country and also abroad. Its purpose is above all to supply information on Jewish affairs in Yugoslavia and around the world, especially Israel. In the 1970's the Belgrade Jewish community began to publish a bulletin of its own.

A Jewish calendar is issued annually, containing the dates of all Jewish holidays and other important events of Jewish interest, as well as statistical data on Yugoslav Jewry.

The Jewish youth occasionally publish their own periodicals, called Kadima in Belgrade and Salom in Sarajevo. Issues of both appear at infrequent intervals.

From 1954 to 1970, Jevrejski almanah (Jewish Almanac) appeared every two to three years, containing articles on scholarly topics pertaining to Yugoslav Jews and contemporary Yugoslav Jewish literature. It was published in 1,200 copies and distributed to various Jewish and other libraries in Yugoslavia and elsewhere.

The Federation also sponsors publication of books pertaining to Yugoslav Jewish history, the Holocaust and special events in Jewish life. Among the volumes that have appeared (in Serbo-Croatian) are: Crimes of the Fascist Occupiers and their Collaborators against the Jews in Yugoslavia (1952), A Short History of the Jewish People by Simon Dubnow (1962), Old Jewish Art in Palestine by Dr. Vidosava Nedomaeki, curator of the Jewish Historical Museum

35

(1964), and The Sephardim in Bosnia by Dr. Moric Levi (1969), as well as several special commemorative editions.

With the exception of two kindergartens, no facilities for formal Jewish education have existed in post-war Yugoslavia. These kindergartens operated in Belgrade and Zagreb since the 1950's under the auspices of the Jewish community. The teachers for the most part had some specialized training. The regular kindergarten curriculum was supplemented with Hebrew children's songs and stories and special programs for Hannukah and Purim. Both kindergartens were relatively small, containing only a few dozen children at last count. They were considered among the best kindergartens in Yugoslavia. The proportion of Jewish children attending these schools, however, was extremely low; the overwhelming majority of those enrolled were not Jewish. The reason for this phenomenon was apparently to some extent geographic. The kindergartens were situated in the center of town, not in the areas where most young Jewish families live. Jewish parents seemed to feel that it was more convenient to send their children to other schools nearer their homes.

Aside from these two kindergartens, which scarcely fill any very useful Jewish educational role, the community concentrates its educational efforts on children's, youth and student club meetings, and, especially, on its summer camp. Special programs are organized for children, often by the women's sections, on the occasion of Jewish holidays such as Hannukah, Purim, and Tu B'shvat. Much attention, however, is concentrated on the student organizations.

The most important activity of the Yugoslav Jewish community on behalf of the younger generation is the annual summer camp. This camp has existed in one form or another since the 1950's. Approximately

36

300 Jewish youth, divided into three age groups, used to spend about two weeks each at a community-sponsored camp, usually located somewhere along the Adriatic coast. In the 1970's, however, somewhat fewer children attended. Along with sports, hikes, excursions and other typical camp activities, this camp tries to provide a Jewish cultural atmosphere for the youth by offering a fairly wide range of lectures, talks and discussions on Jewish subjects, such as the Bible, Jewish history and current Jewish problems. This cultural emphasis is most apparent among the oldest group (those over 17). The program is conducted by the Federation and the communal leadership, along with some Israelis. A number of Jewish youth from other Eastern and Western European countries also take part. The camp experience provides many Jewish youth, especially those from the smaller communities, with their only real contact with Jewish life and the opportunity to meet other young Jews. The effectiveness of this activity is difficult to evaluate, but it does help to provide some Jewish awareness.

Summer vacations have also been used by the community to foster closer ties among members of the older and middle generations. For a number of years, a group of from 60 to 100 communal functionaries and activists from all over the country spent two to three weeks together on the Italian seacoast. They engaged in joint cultural as well as social activities. For the so-called "middle generation" from 25 to 45, smaller group vacations for the entire family have been attempted on several occasions but with less success. All three summer programs are run by the Federation.

The community perceives as its greatest responsibility the development of Jewish consciousness among the younger generation. This task is particularly difficult, due to the lack of educational facilities and qualified personnel as well as the absence of traditional Jewish observance patterns within the society. Stress is placed on the cultural rather than the religious aspects of the Jewish experience.

Each of the larger local communities has its own youth or student club which meets regularly and sponsors cultural and social programs. These meetings are usually popular and well attended. Youth activities are organized by a Coordinating Committee for Youth made up of club presidents, with the help of the Federation, which sponsors special youth leadership seminars. Aside from the summer program, there have also been annual countrywide youth gatherings in November and a small Macabiada (sports competition) in the spring in which all the clubs have participated. In addition, during the 1960's and 1970's Jewish young people attended an annual summer seminar for six weeks in Israel, usually held at Kibbutz Gat, which has a large number of residents from Yugoslavia. The Yugoslav student clubs often send representatives to European and American conferences of Jewish youth.

After World War II, the Jewish community in Yugoslavia, with the help of the American Jewish Joint Distribution Committee, set up a wide network of social welfare institutions to help the poor, the orphaned, the sick and the elderly in their recovery from the devastations of the war. These facilities, which included orphanages, old age homes, clinics, soup kitchens and student mensas were administered by the Autonomous Committee for Aid, which operated from 1948 to 1952. When life became more settled and a majority of Yugoslav Jewish survivors left for Israel, these institutions were no longer needed and were gradually phased out.

The most important social service institution functioning within the Yugoslav Jewish community today is the Home for the Aged in Zagreb. This home has existed in one form of another since 1980. Today it is housed in a new, modern building, which can accommodate 115 persons. It has its own synagogue, in addition to all other necessary facilities, including an up-to-date hospital wing. This institution is considered one of the finest of its kind in Yugoslavia and compares favorably with Jewish Homes for the Aged elsewhere in Europe. The residents and their families contribute only as much as they can afford to pay for room and board.

The Home for the Aged was built by the Federation with the help of funds from the Joint Distribution Committee and the Jewish Claims Conference. It is a countrywide institution, run by a directory of 16, including 11 from Zagreb and five representatives of the other Jewish communities. The president of the Home is an ex-officio member of the Executive Board of the Federation.[19]

The Jewish community provides aid to needy individuals, including monetary assistance to those who are sick, elderly or no longer able to support themselves. It has also given help to Jewish transients or refugees on their way from Eastern Europe to Israel.

One of the primary roles of the Federation is the maintenance of proper relations with the state and the rest of Yugoslav society on the one hand and close ties with world Jewry and especially Israel on the other. The body in charge of such matters is the Council for Inter-Ethnic and International Relations, which is composed of the executive of the Federation plus communal representatives.

Fund-raising does not constitute a particularly important facet of Jewish communal life in Yugoslavia. The community is supported partially by voluntary contributions from its membership, but it could not survive without outside aid from such sources as the Joint Distribution Committee and the Memorial Foundation. To the best of my knowledge, there are almost no collection appeals for the community itself, although contributions to the Home for the Aged, war memorials and the community are encouraged and widely publicized.

Collections for Israel do not occur regularly but only on special occasions. By 1955, the Yugoslav Jewish community had collected enough funds to plant 51,735 trees in the Martyrs' Forest in Israel as a memorial to the Yugoslav Jews who were killed during World War II. In 1964, they collected money to plant a forest near Kibbutz Gat in memory of Dr. Albert Vajs, who had been president of the Federation from 1948 to 1964.

Religious services are maintained for the benefit of those who wish to use them. In the major centers, services are held on Friday evenings and on holidays. In all of the larger communities, Rosh Hashana and Yom Kippur services attract a sizable crowd.

These services are generally led by knowledgeable laymen, since there are no qualified religious personnel in the country. The last remaining rabbi in the country, Rabbi Menahem Romano, died in 1968 at the age of eighty-seven. Since then, the Federation conducted an intensive search for suitable rabbinical candidates. On occasion, visiting rabbis were brought in from Israel to conduct New Year services or for Passover. In 1972, a retired diplomat, Cadik Danon, who had some formal theological training before the war, returned to Yugoslavia and began serving as the rabbi for the Federation.

40

With respect to religious observance in the home
and attendance at synagogue, according to the 1971
survey, in Belgrade, 43.1 percent of the respondents
over fifteen years of age claimed to observe some
Jewish holidays and customs and 30.9 percent said they
attended synagogue at least once a year; in Zagreb
(including the Home for the Aged), these percentages
were 51.8 and 38.8, respectively; while in Sarajevo,
they proved somewhat lower, 27.1 percent and 17.7
percent. Of those attending synagogue, more than 85
percent were over forty-five, while those over sixty-
five comprised roughly 50 percent of this group. More
than half of the synagogue-goers were women.
Apparently, there is no direct correlation between
traditional Jewish religious observance on the one
hand and active participation in community affairs on
the other. In Sarajevo, where synagogue attendance
seems particularly low, communal activity, especially
among the younger generation, seems significantly
higher than elsewhere, whereas in Zagreb, exactly the
opposite holds true.

Holidays continue to be celebrated by the
community as a whole. Special programs are sponsored
by the women's groups and the youth for such occasions
as Hannukah, Purim and Tu B'shvat. The major communities also hold an annual communal seder on the first
night of Passover. Matzot are made available during
Passover as a gift from the Joint Distribution
Committee, and lulavim and etrogim as well as other
religious articles are supplied from Israel for Succot
or other occasions. Kosher meat is not readily
available and must be imported from Italy or Austria
if necessary.

Religious life, however, is at a minimum and the
younger generation displays little or no interest in
it. The Federation itself provides only limited support for religious endeavors and stresses the secular
cultural side of communal life.

The Federation is responsible for looking after Jewish cemeteries in localities where a Jewish community no longer exists. Some of these cemeteries have been liquidated and moved elsewhere, while others are being maintained at considerable expense. In addition, the Jewish community has erected close to thirty memorials around the country to commemorate the Jews who died in the war.

Political Dynamics of the Jewish Community

Local communal councils are elected every two years at open meetings in each of the larger communities. All members of the community are eligible to attend the meeting and vote. In general, only the fairly small corps of communal activists take part in such elections, although in recent years members of the younger and middle generations have been encouraged to participate.

Elections are not considered a major "issue" in the community but are for the most part pro forma. There is no party system and there are no obvious factions. Elections are not contested. Only one electoral list is standardly submitted and those who receive the most votes in the secret balloting are elected. For example, in the 1971 Belgrade communal elections, fifty-eight individuals ran for office and forty-three were elected, of whom twelve were women and seven were young people.[20]

The local executive board is made up of the president, two vice-presidents, a secretary and a treasurer, who are elected at the communal meeting, plus the heads of the various sub-committees, who are generally appointed.

These election procedures are fairly routine and the same people tend to be re-elected repeatedly, often to the same offices. In some communities, the office of the president and vice-president are retained by the same individuals over long periods of time. In Zagreb, for example, from the 1950's into the 1970's, the president of the community remained Dr. Leo Singer and the vice-presidents, Dr. Oto Centner and Dr. Milan Pollak. In other centers, there is slightly more rotation in office. In Belgrade and Sarajevo, these offices are passed around among a small group of men.

The leaders of the larger local communities also serve as leaders of the countrywide community, since they participate in the Conference of Communities and are members of the Executive Board of the Federation. The Executive Board is made up in part of persons elected by the Conference of Communities and in part of persons designated by the communal councils themselves. Thus the same people, by and large, control both the countrywide and the local organizations and institutions.

The most authoritative figure in the Federation, its president, is not immediately involved in local Jewish communal affairs, however. The individual who holds that particular office is elected on a more or less permanent basis and is automatically re-elected by the Conference of Communities every three years. Since World War II, the office of president of the Federation has been occupied by three men, Dr. Friedrich Pops, the pre-war incumbent, from 1945 to 1948, Dr. Albert Vajs, from 1948 to 1964 and Dr. Lavoslav Kadelburg from 1964 to the present. The office of secretary of the Federation is also not affected by elections.

The Jewish community is financed partially by voluntary contributions from its members and, it seems, from occasional state subsidies, but it relies heavily on funds from outside Jewish organizations, such as the Joint Distribution Committee and the Memorial Foundation for Jewish Culture. Unfortunately, the details of these financial arrangements are not available. In 1962, however, according to the American Jewish Yearbook, the Yugoslav Jewish Community received $114,000 from the Joint Distribution Committee for welfare purposes, plus $18,000 for cultural and educational purposes.[21] The Federation is in charge of the raising and distribution of funds, although private donations may also be made to local communities or specific institutions, such as the Home for the Aged in Zagreb.

The Yugoslav Jewish community is bound together by its sense of commitment to its own survival. Undoubtedly, ideological differences exist between the older and younger generations, between the religious minority and the secularist majority or even between Ashkenazic and Sephardic traditionalists, but these underlying conflicts are for the most part suppressed in the interest of unity and consensus. Thus, although internally there is probably a certain degree of dissension and personal conflict, the community feels that it must always present a united front to the outside world and hence minimizes such problems. The community, on the whole, tends to stress the positive side of its activities and its achievements rather than its negative aspects and its difficulties. Thus, for example, leaders rarely discuss openly the implications of the extremely high rate of intermarriage, but point out instead that many partners in such marriages and even their children take part in communal life. They also tend to minimize the difficulties they face vis-a-vis the state with regard to their open support of Israel. The community is probably also guilty of a false

44

optimism about its ability to maintain the status quo in the future.

Leadership and Participation
in the Jewish Community

The principal positions of leadership in the community are to be found in the Federation, the executive boards of the larger local communities and, to a lesser extent, in the subsidiary bodies, such as the Directory of the Home for the Aged. Nearly all leadership positions are in the hands of volunteers, with few exceptions. The secretary of the Federation, the director of the Home for the Aged, the curator of the Jewish Museum and the youth coordinator may be considered professionals. It is the voluntary leadership, however, who control for the most part the communal institutions, organizations and decision-making.

One becomes active in the community by getting elected to the communal council or appointed to one of its sub-committees or by participating in the women's section, the youth group, the directory of the Home for the Aged or even the choir. The people most active in communal affairs tend to be over forty-five. There are no obvious differences in economic or social status between participants in different institutions or organizations. The main differentiating factors would seem to be age and degree of Jewish background. Women are often more active in educational and cultural organizations than men, while men and women share the responsibilities for social welfare institutions. Those active in synagogue and religious life are usually over sixty. Otherwise, no meaningful distinctions between types of activists can be discerned.

Voluntary leadership lies almost exclusively in the hands of persons in professional fields. Those in top positions are virtually all lawyers, doctors or professors of some kind; many of them have held responsible positions but are now retired. Most of these individuals can probably be classified as upper-middle class by prestige, if not by wealth.

The composition of the Zagreb communal council casts insight into the occupational distribution of Jewish leadership. In 1965, out of forty-five persons elected to office (including ten substitutes), eleven were physicians, ten were pensioners, ten "employees," six housewives and four artisans, three judges or lawyers and one student. A total of eighteen (or 40 percent), including the president and both vice-presidents, were either active or retired professionals, while ten (or 22 percent) were women.)[22]

Those presently holding top leadership positions seem to have all been born in Yugoslavia in medium or large Jewish communities usually before World War I, and their Jewish family background was generally rather traditional. They were often active in the Jewish youth movement during the interwar period, although few held leadership positions within the Jewish community before World War II. During the war, most of the present leadership cadres were German prisoners-of-war, who had been called up as reserve officers in 1941; others fought as partisans under Tito or found safety in Italian-occupied territory.

A brief sketch of the backgrounds of several of the top leaders should serve to illustrate this pattern. The man occupying the highest position of authority within the Yugoslav Jewish community is

Dr. Lavoslav Kadelburg, the president of the Federation of Jewish Communities. Dr. Kadelburg was born in 1910 in Vinkovci, a town in Croatia-Slavonia with a Jewish population of about six hundred on the eve of World War II. He was active in Jewish affairs since high school, when he was president of the local Jewish youth association and a member of the Steering Committee of the Federation of Jewish Youth Organizations of Yugoslavia. While studying law in Zagreb, he participated in Jewish student clubs. As a reserve officer in the Yugoslav Army, he spent the war in a military prison camp. After 1945, he became a public prosecutor and later held a number of high government positions in both the republic and federal administrations, including the post of director of the Federal Institute of Public Administration and assistant general director of the Federal Institute for Social Security, until his retirement in 1966. He is an active member of the League of Communists and several other prestigious Yugoslav organizations. Immediately after World War II, he began to play a leading role in Yugoslav Jewish life. From 1945 to 1952, he was a member and then president of the Autonomous Committee for Aid. In 1945, he became a member of the Executive Board of the Federations. In 1948, he was elected vice-president and in 1964, he succeeded Dr. Albert Vajs as president. Kadelburg's sphere of influence has always been within the Federation, rather than on the local communal level. As a member of the World and European Executives of the World Jewish Congress and as vice-president of the European Council for Jewish Communal Services (among several such posts), he is Yugoslav Jewry's "ambassador" to the outside world.[23]

Another excellent example of a communal leader can be seen in Dr. Leo Singer, former president of the Zagreb community, vice-president of the Federation and member of the Council for Inter-Ethnic and

International Relations, member of the Directory of the Home for the Aged (formerly in charge of the building committee). Leo Singer was born in 1901 in Zagreb and studied law there. He was active in the local Jewish high school and university groups and secretary of the Federation of Jewish Youth Organizations. He worked as a lawyer in Zagreb until the war, but was not particularly active in Jewish communal affairs. During the war, he was interned in an Italian concentration camp on the Adriatic coast. After the war, he became a public prosecutor, especially concerned with investigating war crimes. In 1945, he was elected vice-president and in 1952, president of the Zagreb Jewish community, an office which he held for over twenty years.[24]

A sample of Belgrade Jewish leadership may be found in Bencion Levi, born in Belgrade in 1906 and brought up in a patriarchal Sephardic family with a very traditional Jewish education. He was fairly active in local Jewish youth groups before the war. During the war, he fought as a partisan. Thereafter, he worked in the Federal Ministry of Interior. From 1946 to 1951, he was vice-president of the Belgrade Jewish community and he held the office of president for two periods, from 1951 to 1956 and from 1964 to 1971. He also served as vice-president of the Federation for a number of years.[25]

These voluntary leaders achieved their positions chiefly due to a personal desire to help the Jewish community in Yugoslavia survive. They did not necessarily need or have any special skills or attributes, such as money or influence. The continuity of top leadership from the interwar to the post-war period lasted only for a brief period, until 1952 at the latest. Thereafter leaders rose from the ranks of those available and interested.

48

The present leadership does attempt to recruit potential leaders from among the younger and "middle" generations. This is done primarily by encouraging the youth to participate more in the Federation and its activities on a countrywide level and by trying to elect some new faces to the communal council and give these new activists some responsibility.

There appears to be a logical progression for activity and leadership from the women's, youth and choir sections on the lowest rung, to the communal council and then the communal executive board at the intermediate stage and then to the Conference of Communities and the Executive Board of the Federation at the highest level. There is extensive overlapping in the leadership of all institutions and organizations. There would seem to be a considerable degree of mobility within this system and it would seem that almost any individual who had such an inclination would be able to rise fairly rapidly within this framework.

The main positions occupied by professional leaders in the community are the secretary of the Federation, the countrywide youth coordinator, the director of the Home for the Aged and the curator of the Jewish Historical Museum. In the 1970's, all these positions were held by women. Although there is no available data on their personal backgrounds, it would appear that the present professional leaders are, on the whole, younger than the voluntary leaders, well-educated but not having quite as strong Jewish family backgrounds. The professional leaders were recruited from the membership at large on the basis of qualifications or skills. They have all received at least a certain amount of specialized training for the position which they hold. The problem of finding suitable professional leaders to perform the necessary functions within the community is great. It would seem that particular individuals are practically irreplaceable. For example, in 1971, Mirjam Steiner, the only highly trained Jewish youth leader in Yugoslavia, moved to Israel creating a vacuum that proved difficult to fill. New cadres must somehow be produced to fill future needs.

The community's leadership is reasonably representative of the community itself. The high occupational concentration of the leadership in the professions reflects the strongly professional orientation of the membership at large, only more so. The leaders differ from the general Jewish population primarily in their greater sense of commitment to the preservation of the community as a Jewish entity, rather than any other obvious factor. Probably the Sephardim are better represented among the ranks of the leaders than the Ashkenazim; this phenomenon may be attributed to their strong Jewish background. Since the community as a whole tends to be fairly uniform in composition, it seems hardly surprising that its leadership should be relatively representative. No particular group is considered automatically entitled to leadership positions by birth or status. Those who had better Jewish education and participated in primarily Zionist youth organizations before the war became the obvious candidate to take over leadership of the community after the war.

In general, power is in the hands of those persons who hold the highest offices, e.g., the president of the Federation and the president of the larger communities. They would appear to possess authority and influence by virtue of their official positions. Former office-holders and some of the older members of the community command a certain res- pect due to their persons, but they rarely wield much power.

Decisions on virtually all matters pertaining to the community and its internal or external affairs are made by the leadership of the Federation. The president of the Federation is by far the most influential figure in the community, but all major decisions must be made in conjunction with his Executive Board, which includes the highest local communal leaders. The Federation leaders make all decisions on general policy, relations with non-Jews and the government, Jewish education and culture, fund-raising, religious affairs and all other similar concerns.

Participation in community affairs depends chiefly on age and interests. The avenues of participation are to be found in the communal administration (i.e., the communal council), the women's sections, the Home for the Aged, the choirs and the youth groups, as well as the synagogue. The communal administration is theoretically open to all, but it tends to be dominated by older men, with only a few women and even fewer youth or young adults.

The women's sections are often the largest and most active bodies operating within the community. Their combined membership across the country was reported to be over eight hundred, of whom some one hundred were considered very active. Membership tends to be drawn from among the older women (in 1968, only one-third of the members were under fifty), although some younger women also participate in its cultural and educational activities.[26]

The active supporters of the Home for the Aged usually belong to one or the other of the above groups, but are concentrated predominantly in Zagreb. The two choirs, which total around eighty members, have a somewhat better age distribution than the other organizations, but participation is naturally limited on the basis of talent and interest. The youth groups

51

are popular primarily among unmarried students, usually ranging in age from 18 to 25. The young people who
are most active in these groups often seem to
disappear from communal life after they graduate or
marry. The so-called "middle generation," the young
adults from 25 to 45 with young families, constitutes
a lost element in the community and presents a great
problem which the leadership has thus far failed to
solve satisfactorily.

Active participation in communal life is limited
to a relatively small percentage of the Jewish
population as a whole. It depends to a large extent
on the degree of Jewish consciousness of the individual and also on personal factors, i.e., the attitude
of one's non-Jewish parent or spouse. Participation
is often brought about by social factors: the young
take part in order to meet other young people, while
the older people are more active than the "middle
generation" partially to combat loneliness and keep
themselves occupied after their retirement.

Women seem to participate in communal life more
than men. In part, this is because there are far more
Jewish women in Yugoslavia than men; in fact, there
were 143 Jewish women for every one hundred Jewish men
in 1964.[27] There are no activities which exclude
women and women are playing an increasingly active
role in communal administration, except on the highest
levels of voluntary leadership. Separate women's
sections exist in most communities and often form the
most active element functioning. These women's sections take care of the kindergartens and children's
programs for the community and also contribute extensively to the cultural and welfare activities of the
community. Any actual division of functions is, however, generally of an informal nature.

Youth occupy a central place in the Jewish
community. Much emphasis and effort is concentrated

52

on youth programs and activities. Students are playing an increasingly important role within the community. Their groups are often very active and their countrywide gatherings number up to 100 participants. Older youths often help out with the programs for younger children. The leadership attempts to co-opt youth into participating in the decision-making processes of the local community and the Federation. Such efforts have achieved only a limited degree of success.

Intercommunity Relations

Extensive ties of both a formal and an informal nature bind the local communities and the Federation. The Federation constantly keeps in direct contact with its member communities through frequent personal visits of the leadership as well as through correspondence. It coordinates virtually all communal activities, including the various organizations and institutions. The Federation formulates the general policy on a countrywide scale while the communities implement its decisions, adapting them to local circumstances. The community as a whole is thus extremely closely knit structurally.

Although several of the larger communities are, by and large, economically self-sufficient, the Federation distributes funds to most of the smaller communities as well as such institutions as the Home for the Aged. Much of the money which is available is derived from foreign sources.

The Federation of Jewish Communities of Yugoslavia has a long-standing affiliation with the

World Jewish Congress, as well as with the European Council on Jewish Communal Services (formerly the Standing Committee). The Federation was one of the founding members of the World Jewish Congress and attended its first congress in 1936; later it was represented at the first post-war meeting of the European conference of the organization in August 1945. Since 1953, the president of the Federation has held a position on the executive board of the World Jewish Congress.

In 1960, when the European Council on Jewish Communal Services was formed, Dr. Albert Vajs, then president of the Federation, helped draw up its first statutes. Since 1967, Dr. Lavoslav Kadelburg, Dr. Vajs' successor, has held the post of first vice-president of the Council.

The Federation also has had close ties with the Joint Distribution Committee, the Claims Conference and later the Memorial Foundation for Jewish Culture, from whom they have received extensive funds on a regular basis.

In addition to these formal affiliations, the Federation and its subsidiary organizations maintain ties with other worldwide Jewish organizations, such as the Jewish Agency, the World Sephardic Federation, the World Union of Jewish Students, the International Council of Jewish Women, etc.[28] In short, it would appear that the community favors friendly relations with nearly all international Jewish institutions, except for those which are specifically labeled Zionist.

The Federation also has developed a network of informal contacts with other European Jewish communities, particularly Eastern European, in the past few decades. Dr. Kadelburg has made several visits to the Soviet Union, as well as to Hungary and

Romania in return. Jewish leaders from these countries have visited Yugoslavia. In 1966, Jewish leaders from all over the world participated in the 400th anniversary celebration of the settlement of Jews in Bosnia-Hercegovina. In 1969, there was a gala celebration of the Federation's 50th anniversary, attended by many foreigners from both East and West. The following year, a large Soviet delegation came to Belgrade on the occasion of Dr. Kadelburg's 60th birthday. Yugoslav Jewish leaders travel extensively in Western Europe as well, attending conferences and meetings of various types. Youth leaders, too, frequently attend Jewish youth and student conferences abroad.

The community does not regularly contribute funds to projects or activities in other countries, except in cases of emergency, such as the flooding of Florence or similar occurrences. Any such token contributions are made by the Federation. As previously stated, the community receives most of its financial support from outside, mainly the Joint Distribution Committee and the Memorial Foundation.

Nearly all the ties existing between the Yugoslav Jewish community and Israel today are of an informal rather than a formal nature. The Yugoslav government severed diplomatic relations with Israel after the Six Day War, but the two countries still maintain trade connections. The Yugoslav authorities have in no way tried to interfere directly with the Jewish community's support of Israel and contacts have never been broken, but the community of its own volition exercises caution with regard to its relationship with Israel.

Yugoslav Jews are allowed to travel to Israel freely as tourists (upon acquiring a visa usually from the Belgian Embassy). Israelis, too, may visit Yugoslavia with no difficulty. Close personal ties are preserved, especially between Yugoslav Jews and Israeli citizens of Yugoslav origin. Yugoslav Jewish leaders make frequent trips to Israel for official or personal reasons. During the summer, Jewish students from Yugoslavia have attended a special seminar, usually held at Kibbutz Gat.

Israel plays a relatively important role in the life of the community. Most Yugoslav Jews whom the writer met consider themselves Zionists, although many choose not to display this fact openly. The community as a whole is pro-Israel but shows it in a subtle rather than a blatant manner. The younger generation are very interested in Israel and often ask questions and discuss it in a well-informed fashion with foreign visitors at youth meetings.

Israel does not officially provide the community with technical assistance, but de facto, Israeli "visitors," many of whom were born in Yugoslavia, do provide assistance in the role of informal teachers or shlichim at summer camps. Israelis of Yugoslav descent form a very important link between Yugoslav Jewry and Israel. They often return to Yugoslavia to see family and friends and they generally keep the community informed of current developments in Israel. The most important formal contact is probably Hitahdut Olej Yugoslavia, the association of Yugoslav Jews in Israel. (Similarly, the Yugoslav Jewish community maintains fairly close relations with the Association of Yugoslav Jews in the United States, which had its headquarters in New York.) Israel does not provide the community with any financial assistance but, on the other hand, the community does occasionally make contributions to Israel, mainly by way of planting trees.

Conclusion

Since the early 1950's the Yugoslav Jewish community has maintained itself intact with little change. It is unquestionably the freest Jewish community in any of the Communist countries, no doubt because of the nature of Yugoslav Communism under Marshall Tito. The community is to some extent limited in its activities, on the one hand, by the subtle pressures that flow from the general disapproval of religion common to Communist systems and, on the other hand, by the official government opposition to Israel, but these restrictions have thus far not proved seriously debilitating.

Tito's death will probably not alter the situation greatly. Of course, should Yugoslavia be invaded--or infiltrated--by the Soviet Union, the Jewish condition is bound to deteriorate. The informal but close ties which now exist between the Yugoslav Jewry and Israel could be severely curtailed and the freedom of activity might be greatly restricted. An outbreak of concerted anti-Semitism, while not likely to be spontaneous, would probably not serve to strengthen or reactivate the community in the long run, but might instead speed up the process of assimilation. And to be sure, any conceivable collapse of Yugoslav federalism, fragmenting the country according to its various national components, would destroy the centralized organization of the Jewish community and seriously hamper its ability to function. Yugoslav Jewry is already in a struggle for survival; any radical change would most likely help to hasten its demise.

The question remains, however, as to whether the community can continue to maintain itself, even in a stable post-Tito environment, precisely because it is so free. Jews are still Jews in the Yugoslav scheme of things--a separate nation in a federation of nations. Indeed, that is one of the community's strengths. But it is possible for these Jews, or at least their children if they are intermarried, to assimilate into the ranks of the nation on whose territory they dwell with relatively little difficulty. With such a high rate of intermarriage and with the lack of Jewish education or observance so pronounced, it would seem difficult for the next generation to acquire sufficient incentive to remain Jewish.

What does seem clear is that Yugoslav Jewry is a community sustained by its organization. It is possible to argue, in the case of many communities, where Jewish life flourishes in home and synagogue, that the formal structure is simply the capstone of a network of Jewish ties, useful to expand the range of Jewish activities and to enhance the efficiency of their work but not critical to Jewish survival, as such. In such cases, Jewish life could conceivably continue even without the overarching framework. In Yugoslavia, on the other hand, virtually all the content of Jewish life is confined to the organized activities of the community. There is little Jewish life in the home and even less in the synagogue. Here, then, is a case of an organization sustaining a community.

The community is small, however, and its members are growing older. The outlook for the future is not promising. Who will take over the leadership in the next generation? Perhaps the Jewish community of Yugoslavia is doomed to death by natural causes. But perhaps its tight organization on the one hand and its will to live on the other will allow it to survive in the years to come.

THE JEWISH COMMUNITY OF BULGARIA
Baruch Hazzan

The Bulgarian Jewish Background

Today Bulgarian Jewry survives as a community in only the most formal sense of the term. In the past, Bulgaria has been noted for its generally tolerant attitude toward the Jews in its midst. Today, however, Jewish communal life has been reduced to a mere shadow of its former existence. The community is kept alive only because the Communist authorities in Bulgaria feel that there are Jews who need to be harnessed to the regime even in their modest Jewish expression. Of the Communist countries having significant numbers of Jews, only the Soviet Union and Poland have gone further to repress organized Jewish expression within their boundaries.

Yet Bulgarian Jewry in its heyday was one of the jewels in the Jewish diadem and perhaps the most Zionist Jewish community in all of modern Jewish history. It suffered from a minimum of anti-Semitism, given conditions in that part of the world. It is the primary example of a Sephardic community that attained its greatest development in the modern era, between 1640, when Bulgarian Jewry was unified under Sephardic leadership, and 1940, when Nazism closed in on it. Ironically, as a result of Bulgaria's situation as an ally of Germany in World War II, its Jews survived the Holocaust with minimal losses, protected by the Bulgarians' ability to maintain their authority within Bulgaria proper and their desire to hedge their support of the Nazis. As a result, the community's effective end came only after 1948 when the overwhelming majority of Bulgarian Jewry moved en masse to Israel in an exemplary display of the community's Zionist commitment.

Jewish settlement in what is today Bulgaria may have begun as early as the Hasmonean period. There are records of a Jewish settlement in what is now Bulgarian Macedonia in the time of Caligula (37-41 C.E.), that is to say, before the destruction of the Second Temple. Since then Jewish settlement appears to have been continuous, at least in one part of the area or another.

The Bulgars themselves, who may have been of the same stock as the Khazars, did not reach the area until the fifth century and did not establish the first Bulgarian state until late in the sixth. In the ninth century, the first Bulgarian empire reached its apogee and the Bulgars converted from paganism to Christianity. During the period of religious disquiet that preceded their conversion, the imperial court at least considered Judaism as an alternative. It is known that Jewish elements such as Sabbatarianism and dietary restrictions played a role in early Bulgarian Christianity.

From the ninth through the sixteenth centuries, Bulgaria served as something of a haven for Jews persecuted elsewhere. Table 3-1 summarizes the known Jewish migration to Bulgaria during that period. The Byzantine or Romaniot Jews represented the dominant element in Jewish Bulgaria until the coming of the Sephardim after 1492. The latter settled in all parts of the country, coming to outnumber the previous settlers in established communities and founding many new ones. They soon because the dominant element. In Sofia, for example, the Romaniot and Ashkenazic communities maintained themselves as separate legal entities until 1640 when they merged into a common Sephardic-dominated community under a single chief rabbi. By that time many of the non-Sephardic Jews had already assimilated among their Sephardic brethren.

Table 3-1

Known Jewish Migrations to Bulgaria

Time	Area of Origin	Comments
1st-3rd centuries	Israel	First settlers
8th-9th centuries	Byzantine Empire	Established Romaniot Tradition which persisted until Sephardic influx
13th century	Central Europe	Jews fleeing from the Crusaders
14th century	Hungary	Especially after the expulsion of 1376. Settled primarily in Vidin, Nikopol, Pleven, and Sofia
15th century	France Bavaria	After the expulsions of 1394 and 1470, respectively
16th century	Iberian Peninsula	Beginning after 1494. They came to dominate the community in the sixteeth century and gained full control over it in 1640
	Italy	Primarily merchants

Both quality and quantity were important factors in the process of assimilating the various Jewish communities. The Jews of Spain and Portugal surpassed the other communities both by their numbers and by their high cultural level. With the passing of time, the other communities mixed with the Sephardim until by the 18th century only two groups remained--the Sephardic and the Ashkenazic, and of the latter group, the majority also assimilated into the Sephardic community. The remaining Ashkenazic community formed its own synagogues, following its own ritual.

Many differences in customs and lifestyle existed between the Sephardim and Ashkenazim, resulting in frequent arguments, especially until the First World War. In subsequent years the differences blurred and the two groups grew closer to each other, forming joint organizations and institutions. This process of integration succeeded so well that upon their immigration to Israel, Bulgarian Ashkenazic Jews found more in common with other Sephardic Jews than with their Ashkenazic brethren who had come to Israel from elsewhere in Europe.

According to Bulgarian census records of 1965, the Bulgarian Jewish community numbered 5,108 persons, of whom 3,047 lived in Sofia. Bulgarian civil law does not require a religious marriage ceremony and thus it is impossible to determine the exact number of Jews according to halachic principles.

Table 3-2 summarizes the growth and subsequent decline in population that has taken place in Bulgaria during the past century.

Table 3-2
Jewish Population According to Census Figures
and Other Sources

Year	Total Population	Jewish Population	Percentage
1880	2,383,610	18,197	0.65%
1888	3,154,375	23,541	0.75
1893	3,310,713	28,307	0.85
1900	3,774,283	33,663	0.90
1910	4,335,503	40,076	0.92
1920	4,857,528	43,232	0.90
1934	6,077,939	48,398	0.80
1946	7,029,344	44,209	0.63
1965	8,227,868	5,108	0.06

According to the census figures of 1949 the largest Jewish communities were found in the following cities:

1.	Sofia	5,062	persons
2.	Plovdiv	1,220	persons
3.	Ruse	452	persons
4.	Dupnitsa	382	persons
5.	Yambol	333	persons
6.	Varna	331	persons
7.	Vidin	282	persons

A report issued in 1952 stated that 4,259 Jews resided in the capital, Sofia, and that the rest of the Jewish population was scattered over twelve smaller communities whose names were not mentioned.

In the years 1948-1949 a mass emigration of Bulgarian Jews to Israel took place. This exodus was in no way restricted to special ethnic groups or other divisions of the community. Table 3-3 summarizes this shift in population.

Table 3-3
Bulgarian Jewish Emigration to Israel
and Other Countries

Year	No. of Emigrants	Year	No. of Emigrants
1948	13,681	1957	38
1949	19,100	1958	56
1950	1,038	1959	49
1951	1,038	1960	102
1952	463	1961	57
1953	346	1962	64
1954	199	1963	49
1955	147	1964	65
1956	109	1966	82
		1967	7

Thus, between 1948 and 1956 about 39,000 Jews, 88.9 percent of the total Bulgarian Jewish population, migrated to Israel.

In the years following the mass exodus to Israel, there have been few signs of internal migration of those Jews who chose to remain in Bulgaria, except for the continued concentration of population in the capital, Sofia.

The following data are compiled from the 1965 official population census and represent the only reliable figures depicting the Bulgarian Jewish population in the past ten years. There are no details on the number of Jewish families, the division of the sexes, or on family size.

Table 3-4
Educational Background of Bulgarian Jewry

	Un-educ.	Not Finish-ing Primary School	Primary Certif.	Voc. High School	Col. Prep.	High-er Educ.
Active Pop.	4	17	690	339	514	726
Inactive Pop.	72	223	1451	264	492	95
TOTAL	76	240	2141	603	1006	821

Added to these figures are an additional 280 children under the age of seven who have not yet learned to read and write.

The active part of the Jewish population, from the economic standpoint, numbers 2,319 persons, or 45.4 percent of the total Jewish population. Table 3-5 summarizes the occupational trends of Bulgarian Jews. The economic status of Bulgarian Jews is relatively good, thanks to their occupational abilities, which allow them to occupy key economic positions and to advance quickly, despite the limitations set upon them by the Bulgarians. There are no differences in the standard of living among Jews in the various Jewish communities.

Intermarriage is very prevalent in Bulgaria, with the number of such marriages rising from year to year. The older generation shows some objection to such marriages, but the couples encounter no difficulty in integrating into the community if they wish to do so, regardless of whether the non-Jewish spouse converts or not.

Table 3-5
Occupational Trends of Bulgarian Jewry

Occupation or Occupational Grouping	Number	Percentage
Administrators in government institutions, economic and commercial organizations	226	10.0%
Scientists, various artists and performers, authors, etc.	416	18.0
Administrative clerks, accountants, merchants	520	22.0
Engineers, technicians	302	13.0
Medical professionals	145	6.0
Workers in the metals industry	134	6.0
Workers in the garment industry	91	4.0
Lawyers	36	2.0
Twenty-five other vocations	449	19.0
TOTAL	2,319	100.0%

In the eyes of the Jewish community anyone is considered a Jew who was born of at least one Jewish parent and who himself takes part in Jewish communal life. Generally, children of a Jewish father seem to identify more strongly as Jews and are considered Jewish by the Bulgarian community more quickly than children of a Jewish mother.

There is no official anti-Semitism in Bulgaria, but in practice there are frequent direct and indirect manifestations. Other personalities who publicly claim the lack of anti-Semitism, such as Party leaders and government officials, are themselves involved in such incidents. The Jewish community is very aware of the existence of anti-Semitism. This consciousness has created a feeling of unease, since the community tries hard to maintain a lifestyle that would be innocuous and unobtrusive to non-Jewish Bulgarians. The Jewish community does not actively attempt to combat specific cases of anti-Semitism or to counter this growing trend, but rather is striving to strengthen its position against excessive assimilation.

The Bulgarian community at large does not concern itself with Jewish communal life. The mass communications media refrain from broadcasting information on Jewish subjects, such as Judaism or Israel, except to issue censures of "Israeli aggression" or to announce the "success of the Palestinian partisans in their struggle against Zionist conquest." The Jewish community has no influence over the handling of Jewish issues by the media.

In this survey we shall not deal with the glorious past of Bulgarian Jewry, with its organizational structure, Zionist activities, or its educational system. We will review only briefly the years before World War II and the war years themselves, but will concentrate more closely on the relationships between the Jewish community and the Communist regime that has controlled Bulgaria since 1949.

In the years 1934 and 1935 two revolutions took place in Bulgaria, resulting in a large reduction of personal rights and the curtailment of democratic processes. As the regime became more and more dictatorial, anti-Semitic groups grew ever more numerous and the central Jewish governing body, the Consistory, concentrated its activities on protecting the Jews against the growing hostilities.

Bulgaria entered the war in 1941 but Jews had sensed the impending disaster earlier. For years they had suffered unofficial persecution, discrimination, and social isolation. Thus, when official political-legislative measures were introduced against the Jews, no one was taken by surprise. On December 24, 1940 a Bill for the Protection of the Nation was enacted by the Bulgarian National Assembly.[1] Immediately following the inclusion of the new law in the statutes, detailed provisions for its full implementation were outlined. Simultaneously, a numerus clausus was introduced in the universities and in various professions.[2]

Many decent Bulgarians protested against the anti-Jewish laws and measures. Writers, lawyers and other concerned citizens sent their protests to the National Assembly and even to the King--to no avail. Most of these protests were not aimed at the Bill for the Protection of the Nation as a whole, but at Chapter II of the law which dealt with the Jews as a distinct race. According to the law, any person having one Jewish parent was considered Jewish. Only if the Jewish parent had converted to Christianity before the enactment of the law, the other parent was pure Bulgarian and the child had been properly baptized, was he considered Bulgarian.

With the German entry into Bulgaria in 1941, the Consistory decided upon internal unification to meet the approaching dangers, but the ordinary activities of the various Jewish communities continued to function as long as possible. However, as a consequence of the Bill for the Protection of the Nation, activities of the Consistory were drastically reduced. (The central Jewish body did not resume any real measure of power until the end of 1944, and even then it operated only on a limited basis.) After it had failed in its efforts to help defeat the Bill for the Protection of the Nation, the Consistory devoted much of its work to trying to prevent or delay the deportation of the Jews to Nazi extermination camps.

The first stage of the deportation plan--the transfer of all the Jewish inhabitants of the nation's capital to a rural center--was carried out. Moreover, most of the Jewish men were sent to labor camps where they were forced to pave roads under the most difficult conditions. But the opposition that arose from all sectors of Bulgarian society to actual deportation to other lands prevented the Germans from carrying out the rest of their plan, so that only about 15,000 Jews from German-occupied Macedonia were deported.[3]

The Jewish youth during the war found themselves confined to social and spiritual ghettoes, isolated from any economic or professional prospects. Their frustration and rage against the Bulgarian government led them to join the resistance movement. When the underground newspaper of the Bulgarian Communist party, Rabotnichesko Delo, appealed to the Jewish youth to join the guerillas, hundreds responded. More than 400 Jewish partisans participated in the struggle against fascism and seventy-four of them lost their lives.[4] Those who joined the ranks of the partisans (and the Communist party) later became the leaders of the post-war Bulgarian Jewish community.

Following the German retreat from Russia, the attitude towards Jews softened and many of the provisions of the Law for the Protection of the Nation were lifted. On November 5, 1943, Jews were even permitted to return to Sofia. Emigration to Palestine was tacitly encouraged. The Law for the Protection of the Nation was abolished on August 17, 1944. The Commissariat for Jewish Affairs (established on August 28, 1942) had ceased to function even earlier, but it was officially abolished only on August 29, 1944.[5]

On September 9, 1944, the Red Army entered Sofia. A new government, dominated by the pro-Communist Fatherland Front, was formed. One of its first acts was to confirm the abolition of all anti-Jewish laws and provisions.

After nullifying the anti-Jewish laws,[6] the government entrusted a Jew, Isaac Frances, with the liquidation of the Commissariat for Jewish Affairs. The classification and scrutiny of the Commissariat's documents, as well as the examination of various financial matters pertaining to the Commissariat, occupied Mr. Frances and his assistants for more than six months. The archives were transferred to the Central Jewish Consistory, as were the 30 million Bulgarian leva (the 1979 exchange rate was 1.65 leva to $1 US) found in the Commissariat's account. Later, the Consistory returned the sum to the Bulgarian Jews. The return of Jewish property to its former owners and the implementation of the various compensation measures introduced by the Bulgarian government continued until the end of 1946.[7]

The fascist regime brought the functioning of Jewish institutions to a virtual halt, but the Zionist leaders of the Bulgarian Jewish community survived the war and were ready to resume their activities and reorganize the cultural, social and religious life of the 45,000 members of the community.[8] But they failed to take into consideration the fact that the new Fatherland Front government was in fact a Communist one, and, as such, would not tolerate any political, social or cultural configurations not dominated by the Communist Party. Consequently, if the first step of the new government was to abolish the discriminatory anti-Jewish legislation, its second step was to subjugate the administration of the Jewish communities. Pro-Communist members of the local Jewish communities demanded the resignation of the Zionist leadership, appointing themselves as leaders instead. While this was done peacefully in most cases, in some instances weapons were displayed (though not used) to convince the Zionist leaders to comply with the new situation.[9]

The takeover of the Jewish communities by the Jewish Communists can be seen as a deliberate act of the Bulgarian government. The seizures were not sporadic, but a well-planned campaign, taking place simultaneously in every local Jewish community in Bulgaria. Furthermore, the ousting of the Zionist leaders and their replacement by Communists was only a part of a broader scheme aimed at the complete reorganization of the administrative structure of the Bulgarian Jewish community. An entirely new institution, the Central Jewish Committee of the Fatherland Front, was created. This committee, subordinate to the Central Committee of the Fatherland Front through the latter's Commission for National Minorities, directed all the activities of the new Central Consistory of the Jewish communities.[10] The official and completely Communist-oriented organ of the Consistory was the newspaper Evreisky Vesty, whose first issue appeared on October 30, 1944. After emphasizing that the Consistory was the executive organ of the Jewish Fatherland Front Committee, Jack Natan, the Communist-appointed leader of the Consistory, listed the following pressing tasks of Bulgarian Jews:

"a) Jews must join the fight against internal and foreign enemies of the Communist regime of Bulgaria;

b) Bulgarian Jews must disengage themselves from all alien [meaning Zionist] influence;

c) The Jewish community of Bulgaria must achieve unity with all progressive forces and contribute its share in the consolidation of the Fatherland Front government."[11]

On January 8, 1945, the Central Consistory declared the independence of Bulgarian Jews from all international Jewish organizations. The official statement emphasized that Bulgarian Jews were simply Bulgarians of Jewish origin, having nothing in common with Jews in other countries. The Zionist movement was designated as "bourgeois and chauvinist." As a result of this declaration, the Consistory ceased its participation in all international organizations. Simultaneously, a spate of articles appeared in Evreisky Vesty, initiating a campaign against Jewish nationalism and chauvinism. Many of these articles were written by a non-Jewish member of the Fatherland Front.

Meanwhile, the central Jewish Fatherland Front Committee established subordinate committees in every local Jewish community in Bulgaria and charged them with organizing political support for the Fatherland Front regime among the Jews and supervising the activities of the Jewish schools, libraries and clubs. They also supervised the activities of the Jewish People's Communities, reporting their acts to the local Fatherland Front Committee.[12] Thus, in fact, the organization of the Jewish Fatherland Front Committee and the Jewish People's Communities became extensions of the general political system of the new regime.

Thus, by the beginning of 1945, a dual structure within the Bulgarian Jewish community was evident. On the one hand functioned the officially-sponsored organizational network of the Jewish People's Communities, connected to the Central Consistory and, through it, to the Jewish Committee and the Minorities Committee of the Fatherland Front. On the other hand, a parallel pro-Zionist organizational network was created, headed by the pre-war Zionist leaders and linked with international Zionist organizations, as well as certain institutions in Palestine. Though both networks competed to gain influence over Bulgarian Jews, Jewish schools, and Jewish cultural, social and religious life, they both expressed their support for the regime and their gratitude to the Bulgarian people. Both organizational structures published their own newspapers and developed their own activities. However, while the pro-Communist network enjoyed the support of the regime, the Zionists were pushed into a defensive position and were required constantly to demonstrate their loyalty to the Fatherland Front regime.

The Zionists represented an anomaly. They detracted from the political monolith of the Fatherland Front and, as such, were considered dangerous to the regime. As a result, Zionists and Zionism were subjected to violent attacks by Evreisky Vesty and the regular Bulgarian press.

Nevertheless, the Zionist Organization developed broad activities, which were neither directed nor even supervised by the authorities. Youth clubs, women's organizations, (WIZO), Jewish schools, social activities, and publications all flourished. Furthermore, almost to a man, Bulgarian Jews participated in the activities organized by the Zionists. The authorities knew that something had to be done to prevent the situation from deteriorating further and saw two possible courses of action. One was simply to discontinue the existence of all Zionist configurations in Bulgaria. But this was a dangerous course. The Fatherland Front government was closely watched by official observers of the Allies, and the dismembering of an organization which had openly expressed its support of the regime was risky. An alternative, more elegant, course of action was chosen--the Zionist Organization was subjected to heavy pressure to join ranks with the Fatherland Front and closely cooperate with the Jewish Fatherland Front Committees. The Zionists opposed that solution and strove to preserve their independence.

On April 21 and 22, 1946, the Second National Conference of Jewish Fatherland Front Committees and the Jewish People's Communities was to take place. On April 6, 1946, the leaders of the Zionist Organization dispatched a circular (#7) to all local Zionist committees requesting them to refrain from any participation in the forthcoming conference.[14] On May 2, 1946, however, the Central Jewish Committee of the Fatherland Front was notified by the United Zionist Organization that Bulgarian Zionists were prepared to join the ranks of the local Jewish Fatherland Committee.[15] The negotiations, which had been started several months earlier, were intensified and on May 15, 1946, the concluding protocol was signed. The United Zionist Organization joined the Fatherland Front and was absorbed into the Jewish Fatherland Front Committees.[16] Although, according to the agreement, the Zionists had an equal number of seats with the representatives of the Communist Party in the Central Consistory, Communist predominance was guaranteed by the pro-Communist Social Democrats and "neutral" elements.

The October 1946 electoral campaign was the first instance in which the unification of the Jewish Fatherland Front and the United Zionist Organization was tested. It proved, at least on this occasion,

74

that the parties to the unification did cooperate. Nevertheless, it must be stressed that during the first months, the unification was an incomplete matter. While a large part of Jewish activity in Bulgaria was initiated by the Communists (declarations of support, acts of patriotism, friendship with the USSR, antifascism, etc.), still the Zionists succeeded in surviving and, in part, continuing their pre-unification activities. The Zionist newspapers, Zionisticheska Tribuna and Poalei Zion, continued to appear, as did other Zionist publications.

Soon, however, the Zionists had to comply with the new reality. Since the Jewish Fatherland Front Committees controlled the budget and the income of the Jewish People's Communities, there was little the Zionists could do independently. Gradually, the local branches of the Zionist Organization were neutralized and all Jewish activity had to be channeled through the institution of the Jewish Fatherland Front Committees and the People's Communities. As a result, the Zionists concentrated on one single outlet of independent activity, i.e., the organization of illegal emigration to Palestine, which was tacitly tolerated by the Communist authorities. On December 2, 1946, a Zionist delegation composed of Leon Strutty, E. Margolis, Nissim Papo, and B. Arditi met Georgy Dimitrov, the Bulgarian Prime Minister and leader of the Communist Party. The Prime Minister clarified for them that all Bulgarian Jews were free to emigrate, a confirmation of a situation already in existence for two years. (A Palestinian Committee had functioned since 1945, organizing the emigration of Bulgarian Jews to Palestine.)

By 1947, the activity of the United Zionist Organization ceased almost completely. The Communists, with their majority in the Central Consistory organs and the local People's Communities, controlled all Jewish activity in Bulgaria. The

75

Zionist leaders tried several times to approach the Bulgarian authorities, but the request for an official meeting with any Communist leader was always denied.[19] The only alternative was to try to deal with the Jewish Communists. A decisive meeting between Zionists and leaders of the Central Jewish Committee of the Fatherland Front took place at the beginning of October 1947,[20] at which time Jack Natan, the leader of the Jewish Communists, made plain the position of the Jewish Fatherland Front Committee vis-a-vis Zionism in very blunt terms. The Zionists were accused of double standards and of a hypocritical attitude toward the Communist regime.

The implications were clear—Zionism in Bulgaria was doomed. New pressure was applied to force the United Zionist Organization into discontinuing its women's and youth organizations. Each of these groups wrote an official letter to its parallel Communist organization, explaining its activities, goals, and principles and pointing out its loyalty to the regime, the USSR and Communism at large.[21] This was one more hopeless attempt. On November 23, 1947, Evreisky Vesty officially demanded that all public Jewish organizations such as youth, women's sports associations, etc., be merged with their parallel Fatherland Front organizations.

On January 19, 1948, less than two months after the Evreisky Vesty article, representatives of the Zionist Youth Organization met with Shlomo Shamli (one of the Jewish Central Fatherland Front Committee's leaders) and announced the dissolution of their organization.[22] The delegation also stressed that former members of the Zionist Youth Organization would join the Fatherland Front. Other Zionist organizations soon complied with the rule and also merged with the Fatherland Front.[23]

Jewish religion was also to be subjugated. Until 1948, the Chief Rabbi had succeeded in walking a tightrope and continued providing Bulgarian Jews with full religious services. However, in March 1948, he was accused of having made reference to the ruins of the Temple in Jerusalem, which was interpreted as having dangerous political connotations.[24]   Dr. Hananel responded with a long, humble letter, in which he called himself "a faithful servant of the Fatherland Front."[25]   However, he, too, understood that the days of independent Jewish life in Bulgaria were over. From that point onwards, the Rabbi did indeed become a faithful servant of the regime--a fact which did not prevent the authorities from imprisoning him in 1962.

Jewish education was also on the verge of destruction. Already in October 1946, Hebrew was replaced by Bulgarian as the language in which subjects were to be taught.[26]   In addition, the curriculum of Jewish schools was modified to conform with the regular curriculum of the Bulgarian public schools,[27] heralding the end of Jewish educational autonomy. The number of schools and students declined considerably: compared with pre-war days, the number of elementary Jewish schools fell from approximately twenty-three to twelve, the number of high schools from six to four, and the number of students from about 3,000 to less than 1,700.[28]

These developments took place at a very significant period. The pressure on Bulgarian Zionists reached its climax after the United Nations Organization decided to establish an independent Jewish state in November 1947. It was this fact, apparently, that prompted anti-Zionist activities in Bulgaria and intensified the "communization" of Jewish life there. As long as there had been no Jewish state, there had been no danger of double loyalty. Upon the establishment of the State of Israel, the

Communist regime of Bulgaria was presented with a dilemma. It seems that a decision was reached to let all Bulgarian Jews emigrate freely to Israel but to force those who decided to remain into total compliance with the requirements and needs of the Communist regime.

On July 9, 1948, Chaim Keshales, one of the main functionaries of the Bulgarian Palestinian Committee received the following cablegram:

"You are authorized provisionally to issue on our behalf visas to emigrants and tourists. Visas should bear the stamp <u>Medinat Yisrael-Misrad Haaliyah</u> (State of Israel-Immigration Office) in Hebrew and French. Validity three months. Further regulations follow."[29]

Mr. Keshales was also appointed by the Israeli Government as Chief Emigration Officer--a post he held until his own emigration in 1949. However, the Central Consistory soon took charge of all emigration, dependent on the Bulgarian government.[30] A Palestinian, and later an Israeli, committee continued to operate for several months. Its functions were soon taken over by the Israeli Embassy in Sofia.[31] Emigration received new impetus after the establishment of Israel, and in less than a year the bulk of the Bulgarian Jewish community had left for Israel. The mass emigration was, in fact, assisted by the Communist authorities, who were well paid by the Israeli government for each Jew permitted to leave.

On May 28, 1949, there were only 9,695 Jews remaining in Bulgaria,[32] and their number continued to drop as more left for Israel.

The emigration was accompanied by the total disappearance of all Jewish institutions in Bulgaria. Jewish schools were closed for lack of students; Jewish economic cooperative enterprises were closed;

Jewish hospitals and other medical establishments were transferred to the Bulgarian government.

Those institutions which were permitted to continue their activity, such as libraries, had to comply with official Communist ideology. A new concept--"cultural autonomy"--was introduced by the government to describe the organizational and administrative status of Bulgarian Jews. However, there was no connection between the real cultural autonomy enjoyed by Bulgarian Jews in the prewar period and the "cultural autonomy" introduced by the Communist authorities.

By the end of March 1949, all Zionist activities in Bulgaria had come to an end. On April 2, 1949, the Central Committee of the United Zionist Organization sent its last circular letter (#28), calling on all branches to discontinue their activities. This was the final act of organized Zionism in Bulgaria.

It must be stressed that at no time were there any repressive acts against Bulgarian Zionists. The hypothetical question remains whether or not the situation would have been the same had there been no mass emigration to Israel, which naturally precluded Zionist life in Bulgaria. In reality, Bulgarian Zionism was liquidated peacefully--and, one may even suggest, by mutual consent.

The Structure and Functions of the
Bulgarian Jewish Community Today

The various local Jewish communities in Bulgaria are united under an umbrella organization which represents Bulgarian Jewry to the government and supervises the execution of government policy with reference to the Jewish community and its leaders. Until the rise of the Communist regime, the central body, founded in the 19th century on the French model, was known as the Consistory of the Jews of Bulgaria. During the Nazi era activities of the Consistory were minimalized and a commissariat for Jewish Affairs was set up, composed of various government officials. Not until late 1944 did the Consistory resume its independent operations, and then only on a rather limited scale. When the Communists gained power, the Consistory became the "Central Consistory of Bulgarian Jewry" and in 1956 the name was changed to the "Educational and Cultural Public Organization of Jews of the People's Republic of Bulgaria."

Actually, each local community is a branch of the central organization, although each has some degree of autonomy in its activities. The various communities are thus centrally united but each city with a sufficient Jewish population has its own People's Community. No sub-communities or separate groups based on place of origin, ethnic divisions or other criteria presently exist. Except for the synagogue in Sofia, which serves a dwindling congregation of old people, there are no Jewish religious institutions in the country. Similarly, except for the "Organization," there are no other Jewish organizations or institutions.

Every Jew is considered a member of the community, whether or not he takes an active part in communal life. If the individual adamantly protests his membership, the community ceases to regard him as an active member, but even then he is still considered affiliated, both by the Jewish and non-Jewish communities alike. Generally, people who stress their Jewish origins do participate actively in communal life, especially as there is no other means of expressing their Jewishness (other than by their Jewish names).

There is no formal means of affiliation with the community. Every Jew is automatically counted within the community but no one can require his participation. Participation is individual and does not oblige other members of the family. The most effective way of leaving the community is to convert to Christianity or else to deny one's Jewishness by way of a formal declaration.

Nevertheless, about fifty percent of the Jews in Bulgaria do participate actively in communal life. Generally they represent the older generation and children of elementary and secondary school age who take part in summer holiday programs and in different social groups within the communal structure.

The Jewish community and its rights are protected under a general law referring to all religious and ethnic groups within the territory of the People's Republic of Bulgaria. The Educational and Cultural Public Organization of Jews of the People's Republic of Bulgaria is recognized by the authorities as the sole representative body of Bulgarian Jewry. The Organization is recognized as a legal entity having defined rights and enjoying, at least legally, considerable power.

Bulgarian courts at all levels, in accordance with the law, make no distinctions between Jews and non-Jews. Jewish halachic law has never been used or referred to even when dealing with cases that directly concerned Jews. Neither are there any specifically Jewish courts in existence, and the Jews have no jurisdiction over personal status, such as marriage and divorce. These procedures are handled within the regular secular framework of the state.

The structure of the "Organization" and its operational methods are set out in detail in a constitution prepared by a national committee of representatives of all the Jewish communities in Bulgaria and ratified by the government. Actually, the constitution was prepared initially by the authorities and accepted unconditionally by the committee representatives. Legally, the constitution is binding upon the government as well as the community but, in reality this is not the case.

The communities having the dominant role in the "Organization" are those having the largest Jewish population (i.e., Sofia, Plovdiv, Ruse, and Kyustendil). No regional or provincial communal structure exists.

Three different periods of Jewish life can be distinguished in Bulgaria after the establishment of the Communist regime. In the first period, 1944-1947, most of the Jewish institutions existing in the pre-war period were revived. The activities of Jewish schools, synagogues, clubs, political parties, social and economic enterprises, etc., were restored to almost their pre-war intensity. Several newspapers were published, Jewish clubs engaged in extensive social and political activity, Jewish schools disseminated the Hebrew language and culture, and synagogues in every major Bulgarian city permitted the free exercise of the Jewish religion. This period has already been described.

The period between 1948 and 1951 was a transitional one, a period characterized by mass emigration, the discontinuance of nearly all aspects of independent Jewish life in Bulgaria, and the introduction of new forms and manifestations of "progressive" Jewish pro-Communist activity.

From 1951 onwards, two different areas of Jewish activity in Bulgaria can be discerned:

a)   activities supervised by but not officially connected with the Bulgarian Communist Party and the government;

b)   activities directed, inspired and utilized by   the   Communist   regime   which   do   not   differ substantially from those of other minority groups or public organizations.

The first type manifested itself through various Jewish institutions such as synagogues, Jewish clubs, Jewish libraries and choirs, as well as through the celebration of Jewish holidays. The second type involved various propaganda efforts not connected with Judaism, such as protest meetings and demonstrations, lectures, exhibitions, and publications, all aimed either at the political indoctrination of Bulgarian Jews or at utilizing the Jews as an instrument for implementing various Party goals, usually in the field of international pro-Communist propaganda.

From the First National Conference of the Organization (June 1957 onwards), the first type of activity was almost completely discontinued, and henceforth activities of the Jewish community became practically indistinguishable from those of any other Bulgarian public organization.

The main focus of activities had previously been the Jewish clubs. Today only twenty Jewish clubs remain in existence, in centers such as Sofia, Plovdiv, Varna, Ruse, Pleven, Burgas, Stanka, Dimitrov, Yambol, Kyustendil and Vidin.[33] Up to 1950, these clubs were places of daily meetings, celebrations, studies and social life. Each club had its own library with books on mainly Jewish topics, including even Hebrew books. In the Sofia Jewish club, a "People's University" functioned, while in many others, there were kitchens for the poor, as well as courses for adults on Hebrew, Jewish history, etc.

83

Various Jewish organizations such as WIZO and Hehalutz used the clubs for their meetings.[34]

During the 1950's all this gradually changed. The clubs became branches of the official Organization and ceased every activity not connected with education, indoctrination, explanation of Party policy goals, or the celebration of various Communist holidays. Although the topics of the meetings and courses are still sometimes vaguely connected with Judaism or Israel, this is usually for sheer propaganda purposes, as for example, "Lenin, a friend of the Jews," "Impressions from Israel," or "Is there anti-Semitism in the USSR?"[35] But generally, the lectures have nothing to do with Israel or anything specifically Jewish. From 1967 onwards, however, the bulk of club activity, one way or another, has been concerned with condemning Zionism or "the reactionary policy of Israeli government in the Middle East." Thus, in November 1968, "The reactionary essence of Zionism" was the theme of a lecture delivered at every single branch for the entire month.[36]

After every important decision of the Bulgarian Communist Party or government there is a new impetus for activity. For months thereafter, all the branches explain these new developments to their members. The lecturers at these occasions are usually sent by the Communist authorities and generally are not Jewish.[37]

Two groups coordinate the activity of the branches: the executive board of the Organization in Sofia and the local Party or Fatherland Front authorities. But since both are instructed and directed by the same source, viz. the higher Party organs, it can safely be stated that the entire program of the branches is determined by the Party and then supervised by its local organs and the Organization's board.

Since all the branches conform to the identical plan and pursue the same goals, the same lectures and meetings are to be found in all areas. The lecturer is usually sent through the Sofia branch to visit all local branches. If the event is connected with some local development or celebration, such as the memorial day of some local hero, the intiative comes from the local Party or Fatherland Front organs. The same lecturers will then visit all the public organizations in the city and deliver the identical lecture. Hence, no difference is to be noted between a lecture delivered at the local branch of the youth organization or branch of the Jewish Organization.[38]

The function of the Jewish clubs as centers of study has been preserved--albeit in a somewhat different fashion. Today, the branches of the Organization are centers for the study of Party history, Marxism, Leninism, and so forth.

Anything even remotely connected with Israel, Zionist history, or Jewish tradition is taboo. In some branches, there are courses for foreign languages, but one would look in vain for Hebrew among those languages studied at the branches of the Educational and Cultural Public Organization of Jews of the People's Republic of Bulgaria.[39]

Although adults are the main focus of attention of the branches of the Organization, the youth are not completely ignored. Special summer camps for Jewish children used to operate, but following the decision of the Organization to discontinue all improper activities, they were discontinued. But at least at the Sofia branch of the Organization, there are music lessons and language courses for Jewish children.

The Jewish choir of Sofia is an interesting case. It used to be one of the famous choirs in Sofia, some of its soloists reaching fame in the Bulgarian opera.

When all "improper" activities of the Organization were dropped, the choir was spared for several years. Then, around 1963, it was no longer mentioned by the newspapers, despite the fact that the choir was highly regarded by the Communist authorities and had been awarded several medals and other insignia.[40] At the Third National Conference of the Organization, the chairman's report stated that Jewish youth showed no interest in the Organization as they preferred to be involved in the national youth organizations.[41] After the Six Day War, when the Organization was mobilized by the authorities for propaganda efforts, it was resolved to revive the choir. On November 19, 1970 a special meeting of the Sofia branch was held,[42] and the participants at the meeting--mostly young persons--showed great enthusiasm. It was decided to reconstitute the choir and a registration was conducted on the spot. Forty-eight young men and women registered and a rehearsal was conducted immediately after the meeting.[43] This somewhat discredits the claim that the Jewish youth is indifferent to the activities of the Educational and Cultural Public Organization of the Jews of the People's Republic of Bulgaria.

Yet another instrument of indoctrination is the celebration of Jewish holidays. Immediately after the establishment of the Fatherland Front regime, it was announced that "all Jewish national holidays will be celebrated freely" by the Jewish community of Bulgaria,[44] and until 1950, all the holidays were celebrated without any intervention or disturbance by the authorities. Fitting ceremonies took place in every synagogue and Jewish club. The consolidation of the Communist regime, as well as the mass emigration to Israel, fundamentally transformed the celebration of Jewish holidays in Bulgaria. It became forbidden to observe certain holidays (Pesach, Rosh Hashana), while others received proper socio-ideological explanations. And now, the only two holidays whose

86

"celebration" is permitted--in a way--are Purim ("a rebellion of the oppressed Jews against the monarch and his clique")[45] and Hannukah ("an epic of the resistance against foreign invasion, in which the Maccabees carried the banner of national freedom and independence, a banner which has also inspired the Jewish members of the Communist Party in their struggle").[46] The religious connotations of both holidays have been denied. Furthermore, the Zionists were accused of having tried in the past to assign religious content to Hannukah and, by doing so, diminishing and distorting "the progressive-revolutionary essence of the holiday."[47]

The two holidays which are allowed are celebrated in one of two ways: either by a dance for Jews and non-Jews or in connection with a "progressive" socialist holiday (with an appropriate accompanying lecture). The tendency is to keep the children away from these celebrations. Thus an announcement of the Hannukah celebration in 1957 explicitly stated that children would not be permitted to attend.[48] Stripped of all religious or national significance, completely sterilized both socially and politically, the celebration of Purim and Hannukah in Bulgaria became "yet another instrument of communist reeducation."[49]

In place of the "reactionary Jewish holidays," the authorities have introduced many holidays originating in the world Communist movement and the "proletarian history" of Bulgaria. Communist leaders such as Lenin, Marx, etc., are annually celebrated, as are anniversaries of Communist historical significance. It is somewhat incongruous to see the Educational and Cultural Public Organization of Jews of the People's Republic of Bulgaria commemorating the birthday of an anti-Semite such as the late Bulgarian humorist, Aleko Konstantinov, but the celebration is an annual affair. Konstantinov is considered a progressive writer.[50] Israel's Independence Day was celebrated only during the first two years of the existence of the Jewish state. Jewish authors, except for Sholem Aleichem, whom the USSR has proclaimed a "progressive author," are ignored.

The transformation of the Bulgarian Jewish community into an obedient tool of the Communist regime of that country was signalled by the national conferences of the Jewish People's Communities. It was at these conferences, or at the specially convened plenums of the Central Consistory, that the official policy concerning the Jewish community of Bulgaria was announced. The various meetings of the administrative bodies of Bulgarian Jews were, and are, no more than appropriate occasions to announce policy, which has been pre-determined elsewhere, usually by the Bulgarian Communist Party Politburo or by one of the authorities dealing with national minorities and subordinate to the Party.

While the first two conferences of the Jewish Fatherland Front committees (described previously) involved only a section of Bulgarian Jews--the majority of whom were involved in the Zionist organization--the third National Conference, which took place at the demise of Zionism in Bulgaria, was a more encompassing affair. It decided to "broaden the functions of the Central Consistory."[54] However, the expansion of these functions was very selective. The cultural-educational tasks of the Consistory were widened and amplified (i.e., the politico-indoctrinational activity of the Consistory among the Jews received a new impetus), while the social activities of the Consistory were curtailed to a mere distribution of aid (clothes and food) for the needy. Ties with "progressive Jewish circles abroad" were also strengthened.[55]

The clause of the Bulgarian constitution demanding the separation of religion and state was

88

applied. The synagogues, previously maintained and run by the local Jewish communities, were separated from these communities and subordinated to the Rabbinical Institute, which was closely supervised by Bulgarian authorities.

The Third National Conference of the People's Jewish Communities was followed, as has been described, by the systematic extinction of the entire Zionist organizational network in Bulgaria and the abolishment of its cultural and social functions. Some of these functions were transferred to the Bulgarian government, while others, along with much of the Zionist organization's property, went to the Central Consistory, "the only representative organization of the Bulgarian Jews."[56]

Three years elapsed before the National Conference of the Bulgarian Jewish People's Communities was again convened in March 1951. The Fourth Conference signified yet another limitation of the activities and budgets of the various official Jewish institutions. Further cuts were made at a plenary session in 1952. The 1952 budget demonstrates a very conspicuous trend, namely allotting considerable sums to various cultural-educational institutions, with only about 5 percent of the total sum going for religious activity. Furthermore, it was clearly stated that the budget reflected "the continuous process of incorporating the Jewish population of Bulgaria into the educational and political institutions of the entire Bulgarian people."[57] There is little doubt that the 1952 reduction in the budget was aimed--among other things--at encouraging that process.

The Fifth National Conference of the Jewish People's Communities took place on April 20, 1952. It was reported that as of December 31, 1951, there were 7,676 Jews in Bulgaria, of whom 4,259 lived in Sofia.

Since the emigration to Israel was still going on and the total number of Jews in Bulgaria continued to decline, it was decided to liquidate the Jewish communities in towns in which there were less than fifty Jews.[58]

One of the few remaining Jewish institutions, the ORT technical school in Sofia, was transferred to the official authorities. At the conferences it was stressed that because only 109 of the 261 students were Jewish, there was no justification in maintaining the Jewish identification of the school.[59]

The debates which followed the official reports of the Fifth National Conference were interesting, largely because this was the last time that relatively free debates were held in that forum.

For about five years nothing altered, and the Jewish community of Bulgaria continued to follow the Party line and perform the functions assigned to it by various Party organs. However, the Sixth Conference of the Bulgarian Jewish communities, which was convened on June 30, 1957, soon after the Sinai Campaign, radically changed the structural framework of the Bulgarian Jewish community. As long as there was a separate administrative framework for the Jews (although completely subordinate to the Party), it could be interpreted that the Jews comprised a social, if not political, grouping, different from the entire Bulgarian people. The very name of the local Jewish administrative configurations, obshtini (communities), indicated that these configurations enjoyed some sort of autonomy, separate from other segments of Bulgarian society. This was a situation which could not be allowed to last long in a totalitarian regime. A new framework had to be found which would not challenge the monolith. Its name had to be politically sterile and carry no political or social connotations. Thus the "Educational and Cultural Public Organization of Jews of the People's Republic of Bulgaria" was born.

The Sixth National Conference of the Bulgarian Jewish communities disclosed that the local Jewish communities had "lost much of their content and functions," many of which had been transferred to the local municipal or Party organs. Thus it was decided to abandon the organizational framework of the Jewish communities and establish a new framework, consisting of local branches of the Educational and Cultural Organization, with the exception of the cultural centers in Sofia and six other major cities.

A long explanation was given at the meeting to justify the existence of the Organization at all, especially after the repeated statements that there was no longer any need for Jewish institutions. Once again, the ideological, educational role was stressed, along with the need to combat Zionist propaganda and disseminate information through Evreisky Vesty concerning the situation of the Jews in socialist countries. The speaker, I. Frances, stated: "The Bulgarian Communist Party, which is the ideological guide for the activities of all public organizations, assesses that the Organization's activities are positive and beneficial for the entire people."[61]

Still, there were certain weaknesses in the work of the Organization. There had been obstacles impeding the complete elimination of some improper activities. The anti-Zionism of the Organization was defined as positive and useful. The weaknesses were to be dealt with immediately.[62]

The subsequent plenary meetings of the executive board of the Organization up to 1966 confirmed the tasks of the Organization as stated previously. Much effort was directed towards stressing the historic connections between Bulgarian Jews and the Bulgarian people. Exhibitions, lectures and books were devoted to that topic. It was decided to establish a permanent exhibition of "the saving of the Bulgarian Jews by the Bulgarian people."

Since all financial resources and income of the Jewish community had been transferred to the Bulgarian government, the Organization had to ask for a sum of 20,000 leva for the repair of the Sofia club. The sum was granted by the Ministry of Finance.[63] One should not forget that, in the past, the budget of the Jewish Community—whatever the organizational framework—had amounted to tens of millions of leva.

The Third National Conference of the Organization convened on February 12, 1967 in Sofia. The standard routine was followed. Despite the separation of the Religious Council from the Organization, a delegate of the Religious Council attended the Conference and took part in the debates. From what he said it can be deduced that the Council, too, was mobilized for propaganda. I. Moskona, the chairman of the Council, thanked the Bulgarian authorities for their support and care of the Central Synagogue in Sofia. He stressed that during several months preceding the Conference, the synagogue had been visited by 600 tourists.[64]

Little had changed in the eight to ten years preceding the Third Conference of the Organization. However, a radical change took place after the 1967 war between Israel and the Arab countries. Until June 1967, the Middle East conflict did not occupy a significant place in the propaganda of the Organization. Zionism and the situation in Israel often figured as topics of articles but they were not the central pivot of the Organization's activity. But, in the words of Salvador Israel, "a new task developed after June 1967, when the Israeli aggression against the neighbouring Arab states began. Since

92

then, the unmasking of the pro-Imperialistic policy of the Israeli leadership and the clarifying of our Party's policy towards the Middle East crisis constitute the most important task of our Organization."[65]

At the Fourth National Conference of the Organization (March 1972), eighty-seven delegates participated. Out of these, seventy-five were members of the Bulgarian Communist Party or the Communist Youth Organization (the Komsomol).[66] The participation of youth at the Conference is an interesting phenomenon. At the Third National Conference (February 1967), Astrukov had pointed out in his report that "the Organization does not work among Jewish youth. Young Jews are being educated by the Communist Party and its Youth Organization. There is no need to artificially separate the Jewish youth from their Bulgarian friends. Therefore there is no need to extend our activity and work among Jewish youth."[67] Nonetheless, it appears that the Organization's increased activity after the Six Day War, and the extra importance vested in it by the Bulgarian Communist Party led to the incorporation of Jewish youth in the Organization.

The Political Dynamics of the Jewish Community

The Educational and Cultural Public Organization of Jews of the People's Republic of Bulgaria is governed by a central committee and an executive committee. The central committee has forty members, elected at a national convention of local community representatives, which is held every four years. Elections are nominally free and democratic but, in effect, it is only possible to vote for one list of candidates, prepared by the authorities. One of the convention representatives officially proposes acceptance of the list and the other representatives accept it automatically. A candidate who is not an ardent Communist and member of the Party is unable to propose his candidacy. The executive committee, which is the actual governing force, is composed of eleven members, including the chairman and the secretary. This group has regularly scheduled operational meetings. Leaders hold office for long periods and are replaced only by decision of the authorities. There is no rotation of leaders into other positions.

Local communities are governed by a committee elected at a general meeting of the community members (in accordance with the recommendations of the authorities). Each committee is composed of five members, including the chairman and the secretary.

Sources of revenue for the community include rental fees on communal property and a certain sum provided by the state. Communal income for each community belongs to it alone and is supplemented by a regular sum provided by the central treasury of the Organization. There are no communal taxes, membership fees or collection campaigns within the community. The Central Committee and local committees are responsible for preparing communal budgets and providing the necessary finances. These funds are used mainly for cultural and educational activities and for financial support of the old and infirm. There is no connection between the influence of specific personalities in the community and control over monetary or operational matters.

There is no common ideology binding the Jewish community of Bulgaria. On the contrary, a strong emphasis is placed on the prevention of any attempt to accept any ideology other than the official ideology which is a result of government dictate, but even this is done with great care and on a very limited scope. In effect, the tendency is to regard the Organization as a social club having no political aspects. The only reason for affiliation with the Jewish communal framework is the fact that one is Jewish and desires contact with other Jews. But this is far from constituting an ideology.

The only two instances demanding general consensus are the elections for the communal committees and for representatives to the National Conferences. Problems arising in the community that cause conflicts are generally on a local level and are usually connected with the distribution of funds for welfare and the allocation of communal recreation facilities. It is difficult to regard these disagreements as serious conflicts. Generally, complaints and criticism are heard within the framework of the general meetings or in meetings of members of the committee responsible for a specific area.

There are very few conflicts based on personal background or ideological strife. Governmental demands and requests concerning communal affairs are accepted unquestioningly, even if they harm the community or its members in some way.

Participation in Community Affairs

Participation in the life of the community finds expression through involvement in various communal activities, such as lectures, meetings, parties, trips, choirs, dramatic groups, etc. Everyone is able to participate in those activities that interest him. Naturally, there is a certain division according to age and interest. Youth activities are mainly centered around youth groups, while the adults participate more actively in meetings, lectures and social functions. It is difficult to determine with certainty the pressures influencing participation, but it is assumed that they are no different from the pressures felt in any society--the competitive desire, the wish for leadership, imitation of others, and so forth. On the other hand, the main factor in determining the degree of participation (or rather the lack of participation) is the concern about how the Christian community will interpret such involvement. In addition, there is a strong desire on the part of many Jews to blur the lines of their origins and assimilate into the general society.

Youth does not play an important part in communal life. Young people do participate in various activities, but they are usually school children, while the older youth tend to disassociate themselves from the community as much as possible.

Communal leaders generally have a secondary or higher education and are well-respected socially and professionally. Almost all are active Party members. In general, their economic level is high, but this fact plays no part in determining their participation as voluntary leaders. Indeed, they see their participation as a necessity imposed on them by the Party. Most leaders come from lower middle-class families or workers' backgrounds. Most are city born. There is no connection between a leader's capabilities and his appointment to leadership roles; rather, the guiding factor is the Party's choice.

Any claim that the leadership of the community represents it in any way is ridiculous. It would be more accurate to say that it represents the authorities to the community rather than vice versa. This lack of representation is a direct result of the way leaders are appointed; they are placed in their positions, not chosen by the community.

At the top of the leadership hierarchy is the chairman of the central committee (the Organization), followed by the members of the central committee and heads of local communities. Local leaders are subject to the decisions of the central committee, although, legally, the central committee has only an advisory capacity. Although decision-making is nominally a function of the committee, all decisions are handed down by the authorities.

Bulgarian Jewry, World Jewry and Israel

Connections between the various local communities are not very strong. Actually the relationship is quite one-sided and is felt only with relationship to the umbrella organization, the Organization in Sofia. Aside from the communities, no other local organizations or institutions exist. A very clear demarcation exists between the community and the Organization. Theoretically, the community is an independent entity that has chosen to unite with the other communities within the framework of an umbrella organization, and has thereby agreed to give up a certain degree of freedom of action and independence in order to let the Organization function effectively; in actuality, the community is required to accept the dominance of the Organization. To a certain extent there are informal relations between the Organization and some of the communities, usually on a personal basis or due to the fact that the community and the umbrella group are in the same city, as is the case in Sofia.

Direction of activities, along with decision-making, is centralized and authoritarian. There is no transference of funds from one community to another, except for the funds distributed by the Organization to the various communities as an addition to their budgets.

The Educational and Cultural Public Organization of Jews of the People's Republic of Bulgaria is not a member of any international Jewish organization, but is a member of the French Association of Fighters against the Nazis, a pro-Communist group. Connections with this French group are expressed through participation in congresses, study missions and visits. The only connections between Bulgarian Jewry and Jews living in other lands is, therefore, by correspondence with family and friends. Even in the period of diplomatic relations between Bulgaria and Israel, connections between the Organization and Israel were limited and weak. Diplomatic relations between the two countries were broken off entirely after the Six Day War.

Nevertheless, Israel plays an important role in the life of the Jewish community, albeit an indirect one. Israeli political policy, the situation in Israel and everything connected with Israel serve as topics for meetings, even though they are given negative Communist interpretations. In private, the Jews in Bulgaria follow events in Israel closely and listen to Voice of Israel to the Diaspora. Israel's joys are theirs, its sorrows are their sorrows. Israel's leaders are greatly admired, and there are those who claim that precisely because of Israel many of the youth of the community have returned to the fold.

For public consumption, however, it seems that the Bulgarian government has assigned to the Organization the task of conducting its anti-Israeli

98

propaganda. At the plenary meeting of December 13, 1970, it was reported that there was constant contact being maintained between Israeli Communists and the Organization. The Israeli Communists provided the Organization with "information and material concerning the true situation in Israel." Several press conferences were organized by the Organization, at which this information was put to use.

The Resolution of the plenary meeting announced that the Organization "will continue its work discrediting the reactionary Zionist ideology as alien to the fundamental interests of the Jewish toilers everywhere. The work will continue in order to reveal the aggressive character of the war unleashed by the Israeli war-mongers in the Middle East." Providing the connection between "the Tel-Aviv rulers and American Imperialism" was also announced as one of the important future tasks of the Organization.

On March 5, 1972, the Fourth National Conference of the Organization was convened in Sofia. The entire Conference was devoted to the Middle East conflict in its various aspects. The task of Dissemination of anti-Israeli propaganda assigned to the Organization by the Bulgarian Communist Party obviously increased the importance of the Organization and its conferences. The Party representative at the Conference was no longer some obscure specialist on the Turkish minority or a member of the Minorities Committee of the Central Committee, as at previous Conferences. On this occasion the Party was represented by important officials. Apparently, the Communist authorities were somewhat alarmed by the connections existing between Bulgarian Jews and their relatives in Israel. According to I. Astrukov, the chairman of the Organization:

The enemies of the people are trying to penetrate our ranks. We have always conducted a struggle against the tentacles of those who, under the mask of 'well-wishers' of the Bulgarian Jews, want to mobilize support for their dark intentions. ...Our task has been and is not to allow members of the Organization to be misled by their relations and yield to false convictions. ...We should not allow even isolated cases (where some) succumb to harmful foreign infection by the bacillus of nationalism and chauvinism.[68]

Less than nine months elapsed before an additional plenary meeting was convened on December 17, 1972, to deal with the Middle East conflict. This time two members of the Central Committee of the Bulgarian Communist Party Agitprop department attended.

Astrukov pointed out the hundreds of meetings, demonstrations, lectures and similar activities the Organization had sponsored aimed at enhancing the class consciousness of Bulgarian Jews and explaining to them the reactionary essence of Zionism and of the Israeli government. Also reported were the numerous meetings with foreign journalists to explain the situation of the Jews in Bulgaria. According to Astrukov this was supposed to be a counterweight to the misinformation spread by "reactionary circles abroad."

It must be stressed that it was the Six Day War and its aftermath that caused the revitalization of the Organization, the expansion of its activities, and the increased importance with which it is viewed by the Bulgarian government. Never before the Six Day War had the activities of the Organization been so intensive and so publicized. Never before had it been at the center of press conferences with Bulgarian and foreign journalists, international conferences and

100

meetings with tourists, etc. It became one of the major tools used by the entire Communist world to denounce and condemn Israel, and leads all other Bulgarian public organizations in this respect. When the October 1973 war erupted in the Middle East, the Bulgarian government issued an official statement condemning Israel for starting a fresh aggression against her Arab neighbors. Simultaneously with the Bulgarian government, the Organization issued its own condemnation, preceding all other Bulgarian public organizations, and almost all other Communist groups which denounced Israel.[69]

Paradoxically, it seems that the Organization of Bulgarian Jews persists only because Israel exists. The Organization had been gradually moving towards final extinction and oblivion, and had been stripped of all independent sources of input (which caused immediate isolation from Jewish religion, tradition and history). It had lost its independent functions and goals, its structure was reorganized to prevent any renewal of activities connected with Judaism, and its name had been changed to prevent "unpleasant associations." The same developments that placed Israel in the center of the international scene injected new life into the Organization, creating for it new functions and new goals.

Thus, Israel once again became a major input source, determining--although indirectly--the functions, directions, scope and intensity of Jewish communal life.

THE JEWISH COMMUNITY OF GREECE
Adina Weiss Liberles

Historical Background

Greek Jewry has been organized in communities at least since Hasmonean times and Jewish settlement in what is now Greece probably dates back further, perhaps to the period of the First Commonwealth. These scattered ancient settlements served as foundations for the extensive Jewish settlements during the Byzantine period (330-1304) and as sources for Jewish settlement in other Balkan countries. As Christianity spread, substantial legal and economic restrictions were placed on the Jews, but their communities generally continued to exist. These Jews developed their own variant of Jewish rituals and customs, which came to be known as the Romaniot rite. The Ottoman conquest of the area made it attractive to Jews once again. After the destruction of Spanish Jewry in 1492, Portuguese Jewry in 1496, and Sicilian Jewry in the next century, Jewish immigration to the area that is now Greece increased considerably. In many towns, especially Salonika, the Sephardim completely absorbed the existing Jewish communities, overwhelming their local cultures and customs. Like the rest of the Ottoman Empire, the peninsula and its surrounding islands were transformed into the heartland of the Sephardic diaspora. From time to time, Ashkenazic Jews also sought refuge in Greece--particularly Hungarian Jews in 1376 and Polish Jews fleeing the Pogroms of 1648 who came in some numbers. By the end of the seventeenth century, the local Jewish communities were organized according to regions of origin, following the Sephardic custom of perpetuating the separate organization they brought with them from the towns of their origin in Spain.[1]

102

Until the beginning of the twentieth century, the largest center of Jewish population was the city of Salonika, in Thrace, the majority of whose population was Jewish. Most of the life and economy of the city was affected by the Jews; for instance, all the port activities were controlled by Jews and the port was closed on the Sabbath and religious holidays. Salonika, which was known as the "flower of Sephardic Jewry," was the seat of a rich and varied Jewish culture.

With the advent of the Greek struggle for independence from the Turks, the Jewish population, known for its support of the Ottoman empire, suffered. In 1912, Greece conquered Salonika and proceeded to Hellenize the city by settling Greeks within it. This led to Jewish migration and, by 1919, a solid Greek majority. After population exchanges between Turkey and Greece in 1923 and the arrival of 100,000 Greeks from Anatolia, the Jewish community of Salonika declined in prominence. Even so, on the eve of World War II it had twelve Jewish schools and sixty synagogues.

At the beginning of the twentieth century there were about 10,000 Jews in Greece. The number grew to 100,000 after the annexation of Thrace as a result of the Balkan War in 1912-13. As a result of Jewish migration, stimulated by the upheavals in the region, by the outbreak of World War II the Jewish population of Greece had dropped to 77,000. Their political and legal status was good; the Jewish community had been officially registered at the turn of the century as an association and its religious status recognized by Royal Decree in 1920, in accordance with the Greek constitution. The Jews controlled the markets of paper, textiles, medicines, glassware, ironware, wood, and hides, and were represented in heavy industry, international trade, and banking. A large percentage of the Jewish population was employed in manual labor as stevedores, coachmen, and fishermen, as well as in the crafts.[2] Athens, which had been a minor community during the Ottoman period, grew somewhat as a result of its position as capital of Greece but remained a far second behind Salonika.

World War II practically destroyed Greek Jewry. Greece was attacked by Italy on October 28, 1940, and by Germany on April 6, 1941. According to the files of the Saloniki Jewish community, 12,896 Jews served in the Greek army as soldiers and officers and thousands of others were in special Jewish sections of the Greek underground. In those sectors held by the Italians, the Jews were not badly treated, but as soon as any area fell into German hands, anti-Jewish measures were immediately put into full effect.

Salonika was occupied by the Germans on April 9, 1941. Between March, 1943 and February, 1944, 46,091 Jews were deported in nineteen transports to Auschwitz and Bergen Belsen, 95 percent of whom perished. The same fate befell the Jews of East Thracia and central and eastern Macedonia.

In September, 1943, after the Italian surrender, German troops occupied the whole of Greece, including Athens. Eichmann's deputy, Dieter Wisliceny, was immediately directed to Athens. Due to the heroism of the rabbi of Athens, Elija Barzilai, many of the Jews escaped into the mountains or were hidden by their Greek neighbors and by the Orthodox Church. Still, the majority of the Athenian Jewish population perished at the hands of the Nazis.[3] A third Axis zone was held by Bulgaria. Over 11,000 Jews were deported from this area (parts of Thrace and eastern Macedonia). In all, it is estimated that 65,000 Jews were sent to their deaths by the Nazis, about 85 percent of the entire Jewish population.[4]

When World War II ended, 10,000 Jews remained in Greece, practically all of them destitute. Almost all synagogues and centers of Jewish culture had either been destroyed or seriously damaged. Reconstruction of the community was complicated because of the long post-war period of political insecurity, continual changes in the government and the extended economic crisis that plagued the country.[5]

The Contemporary Jewish Community of Greece

The countrywide Jewish population of Greece today is approximately 5,400 souls,[6] distributed among fourteen to eighteen communities scattered throughout the country. The precise number is contingent upon whether or not official status is involved. A Jewish community having at least twenty but less than one hundred people is not entitled under Greek law to maintain a Community Council of its own but it may hold religious services. A settlement of less than twenty Jews is not considered a community by the government and is not entitled to maintain organized community activities at all.[7] The Central Board of Greek Jewish Communities is recognized as the legal guardian of such settlements. The principal Jewish communities are Athens, with approximately 2,800 Jews; Salonika (Thessaloniki) with 1,060 Jews; Larissa, with approximately 400 Jews, and Volos, with approximately 190 Jews. There has been a continuous migration of Jews from smaller Jewish communities to Athens, accounting for its growth in importance since the war. Migrants are usually young adults, predominantly university students and graduates, who are often followed by their parents.[8] Athens has been the seat of most countrywide Jewish organizations since the war.

In the period following the end of World War II there was considerable emigration, especially of poorer Jews, from Greece. The Greek civil war made emigration difficult because of draft laws, but after Greece's de facto recognition of the State of Israel, a Greek cabinet committee permitted Jews of draft age to emigrate to Israel on condition that they renounce their Greek citizenship. The period of greatest immigration to Israel was between 1945-1955. By the end of the 1950's, about 3,500 Jews had settled in Israel, 1,200 in the United States and a few others in Canada, Australia, South Africa, the Congo and Latin America, notably, Brazil. Immigration to the United States was facilitated under the U.S. Refugee Act in 1954.[9] Since the end of the 1950's, emigration has been almost nil, except for a small but continuing immigration to Israel, especially of young adults who have studied there.

Almost the entire Jewish population of Greece today is Sephardic, although the few Ashkenazic families in Athens play an active role in communal affairs. There are no separate organizations for Jews of specific communal backgrounds. On the High Holidays, however, two separate religious services are held, since the big synagogue follows the Sephardic ritual and is frequented by the native Athenian Jews and the Jews who moved to Athens from Salonika, while a smaller minyan following the older Romaniot ritual draws Jews from Ioannina and related communities.[10]

The Jews of Greece have largely recovered from the economic depression of World War II and the post-war years. In 1945 only two percent of the surviving Jews were totally self-supporting; by 1954 only ten percent were indigent, and today very few Jews receive aid.[11] The Jews are active in many occupations, but especially as merchants and industrialists in the textile, garment, and jewelry industries. Jews tend to work with and for other Jews. A few Jews hold high

106

posts in the civil service and recently some Jews have entered politics.[12]

Jewish enrollment in Greek universities has increased in the past decade, but most graduates return to their family businesses. The Central Board of Jewish Communities, which provided economic assistance for study in Greek universities has recently begun funding studies in Israel as well.[13] Eighty-five students studied in Israel in 1979. Participation in political and ideological activities is pronounced among Greek secondary school and university students in general, and increasing numbers of young Jews are becoming involved in student leftist political organizations, which are anti-Israel.[14]

Greece has a relatively high rate of inter-marriage, due partly to the relative isolation of young Jews in small communities, a lack of enough prospective partners, and growing fraternization with non-Jews in secondary schools and universities. Even the more traditionally identified Jewish community of Salonika has noted a progressive rise within the past two decades, while in the small communities it is estimated that ten percent of the marriages a year are intermarriages.[15] Civil marriage does not exist in Greece. Formerly most such marriages were followed by the conversion to Judaism of the non-Jewish spouse; recently it has grown more common for the Jewish spouse to convert to Greek Orthodoxy. Great concern about this is being demonstrated by all Jewish organizations and the community as a whole. In 1978, the Central Board of Jewish communities organized a trial conversion class for women in Athens. Previously, potential converts attended courses in Canada, Switzerland and Turkey.[16]

Anyone born Jewish or converted to Judaism is considered Jewish both by the Jews and non-Jews. All Jewish weddings are performed in the synagogue and

107

Jewish sons all undergo circumcision. Jewish children are automatically registered in the archives of the Jewish community.[17] Parents in a mixed marriage must determine their child's religion before he reaches four years of age, for required registration for nursery school includes statement of religion. Greek identity cards state the bearer's religion as well.[18]

There is no organized anti-Semitism in Greece and individual Jews suffer no overt discrimination. In the civil war following World War II, some Jewish partisans held to be Communists were imprisoned, but later released on condition that they emigrate to Israel and renounce Greek citizenship. From 1960 to 1963 a wave of swastika painting swept Greece, especially affecting directors of pro-Israel plays, members of Jewish groups or Greek artists who had visited Israel. Cessation of the attacks in 1963 was attributed to sharp and instant criticism on the part of the press, the Minister of Justice, and the primate of the Greek Orthodox Church.[19]

In the past decade anti-Semitic acts and insinuations have taken two forms: anti-Israel propaganda and anti-Jewish theological insinuations. An estimated 20,000 Palestinian and Arab students in Athens and Salonika and the presence of large numbers of Arabic-speaking dockworkers in Piraeus have added to the government's inclination toward the Palestinian cause. An opening was provided for Arab anti-Israel attitudes under the regime of the Colonels and has steadily developed in the present regime. Extensive economic and diplomatic relations exist with many Arab governments, especially the Syrian Baath party.[20] Following the screening of the television documentary Holocaust in 1979 the plight of European Jewry in World War II was frequently compared to that of the Palestinian refugees or to events on Cyprus.[21] An office of the Palestine Liberation Organization was opened in Athens, and Greece was the scene of a terrorist attack on an El Al plane. Anti-Israel articles appear quite frequently in the Greek mass media and are offset only by the local Jewish press.[22]

According to Steven Bowman, insinuating Jewish guilt for disasters has always been approved by some elements in the Greek establishment.[23] Anti-Semitic statements on the part of the clergy represent some of the internal struggles of Church politics, as well as attesting to the struggle of Orthodoxy against invading heterodoxies which have gained adherents in recent years. Thus, linking the Jews to heresies such as Communism or Jehovah's Witnesses equates them in religious terms to the older struggle of the Church against the synagogue. In 1977, a high prelate published a virulent newspaper article accusing the Jews of deicide.

Generally speaking, religious castigations or political insinuations have had little effect on relations with individual Jews. However, the community still remembers the fear generated by the Nazi experience and is careful not to call attention to itself and its uniqueness. Publicizing of Zionist activities or anything reminiscent of nationalism are generally discouraged by the communal leaders.[24]

The Jews of Greece are well-known for their loyalty to their country. They supported the military regime in power from 1967 to 1974.[25] Following the Turkish invasion of Cyprus in 1974 and the subsequent toppling of the "Regime of the Colonels," the Jews have shown the same support for the present government. Between 1945 and 1977 no Greeks from minority groups were allowed to become officers in the Greek Army, revising the pre-war situation. In 1977 this restriction was lifted for the Jews alone. Often relations between leaders of the Jewish and general Greek communities are based on "old-boy" school and social ties.[26]

The Central Board of Jewish Communities, with its headquarters in Athens, is the umbrella organization for all Greek Jewish communities. It dates back to the period following World War II when it served mainly to channel funds from the Joint Distribution Committee and the Conference on Jewish Material Claims against Germany to individual communities and to represent Greek Jews in their official relations with the government.[27] In general, the Board has concentrated on its external relations role and left the management of the internal activities of Greek Jewry to the local community boards. The Central Board represents the Jewish community to the government, army, Church and so forth, as well as in multicountry Jewish organizations. In addition it is the legal guardian of the interests of Jews living in communities of less than twenty Jewish inhabitants. The Board deals extensively with problems of Jewish education and under its auspices educational programs--seminars, congresses, international meetings --are prepared for both youth and adults.[28]

The Democratic elections to the Central Board both in the pre-1967 and the post-1974 years stand in strong contrast to the period of the "Regime of the Colonels." Before 1967, the Central Board was elected by representatives of all the Jewish communities. Each community elected a general assembly, which in turn, appointed an executive board. Representatives of the various community executive boards elected the twelve members of the Central Board at a special congress held every three years.[29]

Following the military coup in 1967, formal elections were not permitted in Greece. Instead, leaders were officially appointed by the government upon the recommendation of the community.[30] The Central Board consisted of five members and five alternates who held official meetings once a year.

110

Elections for the Central Board were resumed in 1975. Every four years each community sends representatives whose number is determined by the local population, to a national congress which selects the Central Board. Elections on both local and national planes are the subject of interest in the Jewish community.[31] Factional rivalry between Zionist and non-Zionist elements at all stages of the election process seems to be a perennial phenomenon, thus preventing a really strong and unified leadership.

In 1967, the chairman of the Central Board was dismissed by the government and replaced by another Board member who has remained chairman ever since. However, it should be noted that the chairman and most of the other communal leaders during that period had been active before the coup and have held their offices in the post-military regime as well. Thus, the routine of Jewish life is minimally affected by Greek national politics. Rather, there is a mutual understanding that the Jewish community can preserve autonomy in exchange for its non-involvement in Greek politics.

Other countrywide organization of Greek Jewry are OPAIE (Heirless Property and Jewish Rehabilitation Fund), the Zionist Federation, WIZO, and B'nai Brith. The main center for all these organizations is Athens. Although Ladino may be used occasionally in Salonika and other northern communities, inter-community meetings and activities are conducted in Greek.

The Zionist Federation of Greece is a countrywide chartered organization with a membership of approximately 750. Defined as a professional group, it was permitted to hold elections even during the military regime. Although once affiliated with the General Zionists, it now has no political connections. For the past two decades the Zionist Federation has remained a fairly static organization, both in

111

leadership and scope of activities. In 1970 and again in 1977 fresh attempts were made to attract new, younger leadership and to revitalize the organization.

The Central Board of Greek Jewish Communities provides some support in financing and co-sponsoring a few activities of the Zionist Federation, but generally there is a continuing unwillingness on the part of the two leaderships to cooperate. It involves more than personality clashes, common as they might be; an ideological difference exists with regard to the emphasis that Zionism should have in Greek communal life, and the fear of Greek suspicions of Jewish nationalism. In the 1978 elections, the incumbent president of the Zionist Federation was elected vice president of the Central Board of Jewish Communities in the hope that some of the gaps in understanding could be bridged.[32]

Zionist education remains important in the community and is partially provided by Zionist Federation tours to Israel. The Federation conducts the community Yom Haatzmaut (Israeli Independence Day) celebration, sponsors appearances of Israeli artists and performers, and runs a Purim Carnival. It has intermittently sponsored an ulpan (intensive course in spoken Hebrew) for several years, but lack of funds and participants have prevented its continuity. In 1979, a new outreach program to small communities was begun under Federation sponsorship, through which 180 youth and adults from various communities met together. The conference was highly successful and it has been planned to hold regular meetings on such a scale.[33]

The Jewish Agency sends shlichim (emissaries) and teachers to Greece and helps direct and initiate activities there. The shlichim also serve as community and youth leaders and summer camp counselors. They have recently compiled a small

112

Greek-Hebrew dictionary and a song book for use in the Jewish school and camp.

The League of Jewish Women was created in 1934. After World War II, women's groups were again formed in Athens, Salonika, Larissa, and some of the smaller towns, in conjunction with WIZO. Immediately after the war they maintained an orphanage and a girls' home. Now the WIZO groups are mainly social and cultural. Among their activities are a Bible Day and bazaar. Three subsidiary groups operate: Young WIZO for teenagers; WIZO Aviv, for young matrons, and WIZO Hatikva, for older women. WIZO in Salonika is perhaps the most active Zionist group in the country.

A post World War II organization working closely with the Central Board of Greek Jewish Communities is the Heirless Property and Jewish Rehabilitation Fund (OPAIE), created by a government decree issued in March, 1949. At the end of the war the total value of heirless property was estimated at between $5,000,000 and $10,000,000. In the first years of its existence, the organization was torn between two viewpoints. The Zionist element wanted a large proportion of funds to be allocated to resettling immigrants in Israel, while other factions thought the emphasis belonged on rehabilitation of the Jews remaining in Greece. The quarrel was voiced in the Greek-Jewish press, and finally the World Jewish Congress was called in to mediate the dispute in 1952.[35]

For many years OPAIE was unable to claim the heirless properties it was decreed to receive, for lack of ability to furnish the required proof of death of the concentration camp victims. Such proof required passage of a special law, which neither the Jews nor the government seemed eager to press for. Thus, for several years OPAIE confined its activities to administering heirless properties, the income of which augmented the funds of the Central Board.[36] In

113

the past decade, the Central Board of Jewish Communities has resettled Jews in small dying communities in hopes of protecting Jewish property interests there. Suggestions have been considered several times to disband OPAIE and transfer guardianship rights to the local communities or the Central Board of Greek Jewish Communities to insure the continuity of ownership.[37]

B'nai Brith in Greece is a very respected organization, composed of quite an active women's section and a men's section which is more of an ad hoc group called together to discuss special problems confronting the community. Zionists are active members of the organization.[38]

Religious institutions do not play an important role in the life of Greek Jewry. Almost everyone attends High Holiday services, but not so much because of religious conviction as from social custom and family tradition. Many small communities hold services only on the High Holidays. In the big centers, perhaps half the community attends other festival services, and the number is greatly reduced on Sabbath.[39] In Athens services are also held on Mondays and Thursdays. The synagogue in Athens, built before the war and renovated after, is located in a less fashionable section of the city, one of the factors influencing poor attendance.[40] In many smaller communities the synagogues remain as relics of past communal vibrancy but contemporary dereliction. The synagogue of Rhodes is used as a tourist attraction. In some communities, like Kavalla, the old synagogues have been torn down or sold and smaller ones incorporated into the community center building.[41]

Most of the pre-war rabbis and scholars in Greece either died or emigrated. The Joint Distribution Committee and the communities themselves tried to encourage young men to study in seminaries abroad and return to serve in Greece.[42] The Chief Rabbi, residing in Athens, studied in France. There are two other rabbis in Athens and one in Salonika. Until recently Central Greece had an ordained rabbi serving the communities of Larissa, Trikkala, Volos, Karditsa and Ioannina, who was a native of Trikkala, in Thessaly, educated in England. But he recently relocated.[43] In communities where there is no rabbi, a cantor or member of the community leads holiday services. In Chalkis and Igoumenitsa (Corfu) local elders serve also as shochetim (ritual slaughterers) and mohalim (circumcisors).[44] It is greatly feared that especially when the leaders of the small communities die, there will be no one to carry on the tradition.[45]

Religious officials are paid by the communities. Most religious activities other than High Holiday observance center around the Jewish rites of passage and on family observance of holidays in some way. Butcher shops in the larger communities sometimes have a counter for kosher food. Mikvah (ritual bath) facilities are available in Athens and Salonika.[46] Marriage and divorce proceedings come under Jewish jurisdiction, as Greece does not have civil marriages.[47]

In the larger centers, the organizations and institutions described above have their local counterparts. The Community Board of each community is the ruling body. Because these leaders have always defeated the Zionist list in elections, subsidiary local groups and institutions have remained non-Zionist controlled.[48] In general, local communities are too apathetic to have conflicts, and when they do arise they are centered on personality, not ideological issues. Communal activities tend not to play an important role in the lives of individual families.[49] Therefore, people who have taken office

115

in any organization have tended to remain in their positions, locally as well as countrywide, for several years, although there is some rotation of offices within the same group.

Community leaders tend to be quite well-to-do; most are merchants and a few are professionals.[50] Women have been playing an ever-increasing role in local affairs in Salonika.[51] Of the twenty members elected to the Thessaloniki General Assembly in 1979, seven were women. Recent elections for the Athens Community Board brought in several young leaders for the first time. A similar trend toward younger leadership was also noted in the elections for both the Central Board of Greek Jewish Communities and the Zionist Federation.[52] Perhaps this marks a turning point in involvement, since a decade ago very few young people were interested in working in leadership capacities and no organized efforts were made to attract them.

Since the Board of each community is a roof organization, it chooses the boards and committees of subsidiary institutions, such as community center, school, synagogue, and camp, if they exist.[53] In the small communities, such as Kavalla and Patras, where Boards do not function, often one family takes charge of Jewish interests.[54]

Table 4-1 lists the functions of the community and the institutions and organizations responsible for their execution.

There are community centers in Athens, Salonika, Larissa, Volos, Kavalla, Ioannina, Corfu and Chalkis. The Athens community has relocated its center at least twice in the past decade, hoping to improve attendance at its activities with a better location. The present complex includes community offices and the offices of the Jewish Agency, Keren Kayemeth l'Israel, HIAS and

Table 4-1

The Functions of the Community and Their Execution

Function	Responsible Organization or Institution
Community Relations	The Community Board (indirectly, Central Board of Jewish Communities, WJC)
Education, Youth and Culture	Jewish Museum, Athens Day schools (Athens, Salonika, Larissa) Youth centers and youth clubs Religion program in the public schools (Salonika) Summer camp The Adult Club WIZO The Zionist Federation B'nai Brith Pan-Hellenic Jewish Youth Movement
Fundraising	Central Board of Jewish Communities
Press	Jewish Review (fortnightly, private) Chronicles (monthly of the Central Board of Jewish Communities) New Generation (monthly of Pan-Hellenic Jewish Youth Movement) Israeli News (monthly of Greek-Israel Association)
Religion	Community Board
Sports	Maccabi (Salonika)
Welfare	Central Board of Jewish Communities

117

the Zionist Center, as well as its youth club.[55]   In 1954, the then Zionist Youth Organization became the Youth Office and was incorporated as a subsidiary organization within the community.   Its main goal is to provide opportunities for Jewish youth to meet, to encourage Jewish identification and education. Activities include parties, dances, trips, lectures, and holiday celebrations. Upon merger of the adult and youth sections of the center, the community hired a director and chose club board members, most of whom were youth leaders.

In Salonika the community has organized a Community Center with a youth club that serves high school students and young adults. Activities include Hebrew classes for all ages, Judaism classes for children not studying Jewish subjects in school, a club newspaper, choir, band, classical music appreciation group, sports, film club, and trips and hikes. Festival and anniversary programs--including Memorial Day for Saloniki Jewry--are celebrated, as well as bar mitzvah celebrations. The youth club is supported by the education committee of the Community Board.[57]

In the smaller communities synagogue and community center are often combined (as in Corfu, Ioannina, Kavalla, for instance). The Volos community center hires a local youth worker to lead its single weekly activity for the community's twenty-five children. The Larissa center provides a social environment for the community's twenty teenagers, as well as sponsoring adult activities. Generally, activities in the smaller communities consist of dances, ping-pong and Hebrew classes. Most of the Jewish youth of these communities attend the functions.[58]

A countrywide Jewish youth organization, the Pan-Hellenic Jewish Youth Movement, incorporated in 1977.

It comprises Jewish students from secondary and university levels, in addition to young people and graduates interested in a Jewish framework for their activities. Locally, the movement is synonymous with the youth clubs at the Athens and Salonika community centers. The Pan-Hellenic Jewish Youth Movement publishes a regular newsletter, The New Generation. In 1977 the movement, in conjunction with the staff of the World Union of Jewish Students (WUJS), of which it is a member, organized a national seminar oriented toward the difficult political issues Greek Jews confront in university politics and in the mass media. The Central Board of Greek Jewish Communities provided financial and logistic support for the endeavor.[59]

A most successful project of the Athens Youth Club and the Zionist Federation is the organization of summer trips to Israel for teenagers and young adults, an endeavor which has continued annually since 1966. Sometimes Salonika and other communities join in the pilgrimage, but often Salonika prefers to send its own group.[60]

There is a summer camp for Jewish children in Kinetta, five kilometers from Athens on the sea coast and about one and one half hours drive from Salonika. The camp attracts about one hundred children from all parts of Greece and provides much needed social contact between Jewish children living in small scattered communities and those of the large centers. The camp directors are Jewish Studies teachers in the Athens Jewish School and its counselors are older youth. Studies are a small part of the camp curriculum, but do provide some opportunity for Jewish education. A source of conflict at the camp is the difference of view between the governing communal board and the staff regarding the place of Israel-oriented activity and expression.[61]

A small Judaica museum was opened in Athens in 1977, in a building adjacent to the synagogue.[62]

About 70 percent of Jewish children in Greece receive some sort of Jewish education, but it is usually very minimal. The Jewish Agency, which has four teachers working in Athens and Salonika, has greatly aided in educating both children and adults. The cost of the teachers' salaries is shared by both the communities and the Jewish Agency.[63]

After World War II, the Athenian Jewish community established a small elementary day school. In 1958 the Joint Distribution Committee (which had intensified its efforts at Jewish education in Greece the previous year) volunteered to build a new and potentially more prestigious school, on condition that a Jewish headmaster replace the incumbent Christian headmaster and that two Israeli teachers join the staff. The site chosen was a fashionable section of Athens, known for its private schools, villas, and embassies. Social status and a low teacher-pupil ratio have made the school popular. About two hundred children now attend its kindergarten and classes one through six. Pupils are bussed to school and hot lunches are provided for them.

One of the most fashionable schools in Athens is the American College. Studies there begin in the fourth grade; consequently, a large number of children at the Jewish Day School leave after the third grade. Several attempts have been made by Zionist-oriented parents to initiate a secondary department at the Jewish school, as originally planned, but most of the community remains opposed. Another school conflict involves the extent to which pro-Israel feeling should be displayed. This issue was especially controversial in the 1960's, to the extent that the directress, who was pro-Israel, resigned and was replaced by a

Christian. Today the only Jewish staff are the Judaica teachers.[64]

Since there are no formal Jewish studies past the sixth grade in Athens except for voluntary classes at the Youth Center, Athenian Jewish children's Jewish education ends at twelve years of age.

Prior to World War II Salonika had a long tradition of fine institutions for Jewish education, but all were destroyed in the war. In 1960 the community opened a kindergarten for children three-and-a-half to five years of age. In 1979 a day school was established, in the same building, presently providing the first two years of elementary school studies.[65] In addition, in four government schools Hebrew lessons, prayers and Jewish history are taught to Jewish students as part of the religious studies program, paralleling the regular religion studies the Christian pupils attend.[66]

Among the once successful but now non-existent Jewish schools in Greece are an Alliance Israelite School, disbanded when it became mandatory for elementary pupils to study in Greek schools,[67] and an ORT school, established in 1948. Subsidies are provided, however, by ORT to Greek Jewish students attending the ORT school in Geneva, Switzerland.[68]

Jewish education in the small communities is one of the most serious problems facing Greek Jewry. Except for the twenty students attending the Jewish elementary day school in Larissa or those in its Talmud Torah after school class, few children receive a Jewish education. An attempt to incorporate children from Volos and Trikkala into the Larissa school program failed. In Larissa, the municipality is taking ever-increasing control over the Jewish school and its dwindling Jewish enrollment. For a time, an Israeli teacher "circuit rode" through

121

several small communities (Trikkala, Kardhista, Volos, Kalkida) during Christian holidays and school vacations. Some educational activities in the isolated commuities are carried out in local community centers, which try to maintain youth clubs. In Ioannina a local teacher gives Jewish religion classes. However, generally, a lack of trained personnel and insufficient educational opportunities both thwart the educational possibilities of many young Greek Jews who show an interest in Jewish and Zionist studies, and widen the possibilities for assimilation and acceptance of leftist ideologies.[69]

The Central Board of Greek Jewish Communities is an affiliate of the World Jewish Congress.[70] Its chairman travels frequently and is able to keep in close contact with other communities.[71]

WIZO, B'nai Brith and the Zionist Federation have international counterparts. The Pan-Hellenic Jewish Youth movement is an affiliate of the World Union of Jewish Students.

Members of the Greek Jewish community visit Israel and many have relatives there. Although increasing numbers of Greek Jews study in Israel, most Greek Jews are not interested in aliyah for themselves or their children. Greece has recognized Israel de facto and economic and cultural ties exists. There is an exchange of consuls between the two countries.[72]

Immediately after World War II most of the financial help given to the Greek Jewish community came from the American Joint Distribution Committee (JDC) and the Conference for Jewish Material Claims Against Germany, (CJMCAG), which began its work in 1945. In the years following the war, funds were used for cash relief, food and other supplies, medical care, child assistance, assistance to widows and or- phans and medical aid to tuberculosis sufferers.

These funds were administered by a Central Relief Committee (OPAIE) appointed by the Central Board and financed through JDC and through allocations from the administration of Jewish heirless property.

Officially, the JDC completed its activities in 1951, but its assistance has lasted much longer. An orphan asylum and a home for young girls were established by the JDC after the war, but the asylum closed in 1949 and the home in 1953.[73] Also a revolving loan fund for short term loans, created by JDC for people wishing to open small businesses is no longer operating.[74] In Larissa and Volos apartments were built for Jewish victims of the 1954 and 1958 earthquakes. The JDC and CJMCAG financed the projects by loans of $50,000 and $65,000 respectively.[75]

In March, 1960, an agreement was signed between the Greek and West German governments, setting DM 115,000,000 ($3,830,000) as indemnification to be paid by the West German Republic to Nazi victims. The original proposal was modified to give greater consideration to Jewish claims, allowing more distant relatives and Greek nationals at the time of persecution, but who had later emigrated and thus forfeited Greek citizenship, the right to indemnification. Of the estimated 7,200 Jewish claims, approximately 6,000 were from Jews living abroad. The DM 15,000,000 paid by the Germans turned out to be inadequate to meet all the claims recognized to be legitimate, and as a result, the claimants received only 55 percent of the amount provided under law.[76]

At the end of 1964, the CJMCAG ceased its operations. Proposals were studied by which the Jewish communities would become self-supporting, through investments. The capital invested would become the property of the community, which would pledge itself not to alienate it. The capital would come from such community-owned sources as funds held by OPAIE and the properties of defunct communities.[77]

Before the war Jewish philanthropists had given large amounts of money to the communities and substantial funds were raised for the creation of many welfare institutions, especially in Salonika. The estimated wealth of such Jewish communal holdings throughout Greece is $15,000,000. Many of these properties were liquidated after the war. For instance, the Saloniki community in 1951 sold a hospital to the government; one-third of the profits went to the JDC in repayment of loans and two-thirds was spent by the community for welfare and grants to emigrants. No central organization supervised the liquidation and proper use of these sums.[78]

The Saloniki community is the main contributor to the Central Board of Jewish Communities, and through it to most of the welfare and building projects of the various communities.[79] The Saloniki community's activities are financed in larger measure by income from its property. There is no community membership tax in Salonika or in the smaller communities, but a monthly membership tax is paid by the community members of Athens. The tax is graduated to each contributor's income. In such a small community, the leaders of the Central Board know the financial status of all community members.[80]

As in the case of other European Jewish communities decimated by the Holocaust, the Jewish community of Greece seems to be in a process of slow decline. Its population consists mainly of those survivors who chose to remain in their country of origin, a few refugees who settled down immediately after the war, and their children. A small community (the whole of Greece has fewer Jews than San Jose, California) with no real prospect for growth, it cannot maintain itself without substantial help from

124

abroad, particularly leadership from Israel. At the same time, it is subject to all the vicissitudes of assimilation confronting modern diaspora Jewry.

Greek Jewish life seems to be following a pattern of transformation from its original organic character to one more purely associational. The Jewish activities of its members are increasingly confined to those organized by the Jewish community and are less and less an organic part of the lives of the Jews involved. This tends to strengthen the relative importance of the organized community without, however, strengthening its institutions, since the lack of an·organic base means that relatively few Jews care that much about the associational side of Jewish life.

The remaining organic ties binding Greek Jews are based on family and friendship patterns, which, because of the character of Greek society, are still strong. In a sense, the formal structure of the community is an extension of those ties and a means to give them better opportunities for formal expression. Its primary function seems to be to assist in the perpetuation of those ties in the next generation. This is a most reasonable task, but without a sense of Jewish purpose on the part of the adult generation, its chances of successful accomplishment are substantially less.

On a somewhat more hopeful note, within the past five years there has been a swing towards younger leadership within the Greek community; hopefully it will provide more assurance than heretofore expected for a continuation of communal life. While little can be done to stem the slow demise of small communities, at least many of their members opt for migration to larger Jewish centers, both in Greece and in Israel, instead of succumbing to assimilation. It is difficult to see a solution to demographic problems

125

faced by Greek Jewry but the community is highly cognizant of its problems of intermarriage, assimilation and lack of Jewish education and is attempting to deal with the issues.

THE JEWISH COMMUNITY OF TURKEY
Adina Weiss Liberles

Introduction

There are innumerable difficulties to be confronted in writing a study of the contemporary Turkish Jewish community. Very little information about it, either scholarly or popular, is published or is available through other sources, whether documentary or interviews with foreigners or recent emigrants. As basic a fact as the estimated number of Turkish Jews varies considerably depending on what the source of information is, and yet demographic estimates represent almost the only statistical information available. Important questions concerning the organization of communal life and its leadership remain largely unanswered. Ordinarily, for the purposes of such a study, a trip to the community in question would be useful, as it would enable communal life there to be studied first hand. However, in the case of Turkey, even such a trip would not necessarily supply the missing information.

The Jewish community of Turkey, whether or not it admits it, is fighting for survival. A small Jewish community in a Moslem land under an unstable political regime which is constantly in danger of being overthrown, it is caught between the hammer and the anvil. On the one hand the general population, especially in the villages, follows Moslem religious practices and identifies strongly with pan-Arabism; on the other, from the inception of the Turkish Republic in 1923, the government has striven for secularization in all walks of life. Consequently the Jewish community is handicapped by its position as a minority

127

ethnic group, often looked upon in the past as foreigners, and as a religious group as well. Moreover,
Turkish law forbids Turkish citizens to have any formal links or even contact with foreign countries or
international organizations. The Turkish Jewish community itself and those agencies in Israel or abroad,
whether government, Zionist or communal, that deal
with the community in Turkey are extremely reluctant
to have its activities publicized in any way at all,
on the grounds that if neither the Turkish government
nor the Turkish people are antagonized, the Turkish
Jewish community might be permitted to continue functioning. The consensus is that the slightest publicity might endanger the status quo.

Historical Development

Although there have been major concentrations of
Jews in what is today called Turkey continuously since
Seleucid times, if not earlier, the Jewish community
of today traces its status and character as a community to the fifteenth century, when the Ottoman
Turks completed the destruction of the Byzantine
Empire and opened the doors of their empire to Jewish
refugees from Spain and Portugal. Mehmat II captured
Constantinople from the Byzantines in 1453 and brought
in Turks, Armenians and Jews to replace that part of
the city's indigenous population depleted by war and
emigration. He granted Jews full religious rights, as
well as the right to own property and to travel freely
throughout the empire.[1] However, the Jews, like the
Christians, were considered foreigners and were permitted to reside in Turkey on condition that the
community pay a head tax for its members, in exchange

128

for government protection. Among other things the tax allowed the community to support a chief rabbi.[2]

Because of the tolerance shown the Jews by the Ottoman sultans, Turkey became a refuge for Jews expelled from Spain in 1492 and Portugal in 1497.[3] With the Spanish influx, the Jewish community grew substantially. An organization called the "Kiahvalik," headed by the Chief Rabbi, was set up, which represented the community to the government.[4] However, friction soon developed between the Spanish Jewish community and the older Byzantine Jewish community, causing a split into two separate bodies, each group having its own chief rabbi. The Sephardim (Spanish Jews) then split into still smaller groups, based on city of origin. As a consequence, the office of Chief Rabbi for the Empire was discontinued for a period of over two hundred years, until its eventual reestablishment in 1936, and control passed into the hands of local rabbis and councils and was often divided among many different congregations.[5]

The Sephardic influx brought scholarship and culture to the Turkish Jewish community. In Istanbul, Izmir, and Adrianople, yeshivot were established, whose reputation for scholarship spread throughout the Jewish world. The first Hebrew book to be published in Turkey appeared in 1494. It would be safe to say that with the contribution the Spanish Jews made to the community, the Turkish Jewish community of the sixteenth-nineteenth centuries was the most creative in the Middle East.[6]

Throughout the period of the sultanate, although the majority of the Jews were poor and uneducated, there were some Jews who reached prominent positions in the sultan's court and with district rulers, as doctors, bankers, advisers, and civil servants. In the sixteenth century the Turkish Jewish community was the most prosperous in the Middle East, but its

129

situation worsened in the seventeenth and eighteenth centuries with the general decline of the Ottoman Empire.[7]

However tolerable and productive Jewish life in Turkey was, until 1839 the Jews, along with other non-Moslems, were second-class citizens by law. In 1839, Sultan Abdul Medjid published a declaration bestowing, for the first time, full equality in matters of life and property on all minority groups in all parts of the Ottoman Empire. Some of the consequences of the declaration were official recognition to the Chief Rabbinate and the appointment of Jews to councils and law courts. Jews became professors and civil servants in all offices of the government. Shortly afterwards Jews were admitted to government-supported schools and modern Jewish schools were also established. Professor Hayyim Cohen states that the third decade of the nineteenth century was the beginning of the emancipation of Turkish Jewry.[8]

In 1855, the community head tax for Jews was abolished, to be replaced by a compulsory army exemption tax, but Jews for the first time could serve in the army instead of paying the tax.[9] During the reign of Abdul Aziz (1861-1876), the High Court of Turkey convened at the command of the sultan to end the disagreements that had been prevalent among various factions of the Jewish community. Once again a Chief Rabbi of Turkey was elected by the entire Jewish community. A commission was then set up, including the Chief Rabbi, the president of the Jewish Community of Istanbul, and other notables to define the status of the Chief Rabbinate. The statute was approved by the sultan on April 1, 1864, and put into practice in 1867.[10] The government helped the rabbinate to enforce the adherence to Jewish religious precepts among the members of the community. At times government subsidies provided poor Jews with wine and

<u>matzot</u> for <u>Pesach</u> even though wine is forbidden under Moslem law.

The Turkish Parliament was opened in 1876 and a constitution was written, in which the rights of full equality for minority groups was affirmed. Jews served in this Parliament, which was short-lived, as representatives of the Jewish community. Nevertheless, the realities of the Jews' position in Turkish society could not simply be changed by constitutional fiat and they were still considered to be a foreign element by much of the population.

In 1908 the Young Turks overthrew the sultan, Abdul Hamid. Jews participated actively in this uprising. Gedalya Abulafia was a minister in the revolutionary government and the Parliament of 1908 included Jewish representatives of the Jewish community. This phenomenon was exceptional, not only in Turkey but throughout the Middle East, where Jews hardly ever entered political life, either because they were excluded from Moslem-oriented parties or because they were afraid to show affiliation to any group lest the constant change in party or factional supremacy affect them adversely. This fear persists and explains why Jews are not active in politics today, and why they never tried to become active in the cause of Jewish nationalism.[11]

After the revolution, military service became obligatory for Jews (1909), a duty which the Chief Rabbi willingly supported. Provisions were made for kosher food and Sabbath observance in the army.[12]

Except for minor incidents of conflict between Jews and Moslems, the Jews in Turkey during the second half of the nineteenth century and the beginning of the twentieth enjoyed good relations, albeit limited ones, with the majority culture. The major exception was in the area of Turkish Kurdistan, where Jews were persecuted by Kurdish Moslems until the end of the nineteenth century. However, throughout this period, Jewish-Christian relations deteriorated. The Christians, especially the Greek Orthodox faction in Izmir, resorted to repeated blood libels. Professor A. Galanté lists forty-eight separate cases, eleven of which occurred in Izmir and seven in Istanbul. Usually the government tried to protect the Jews in such circumstances.[13]

During World War I, the Jews of Istanbul prospered greatly. This fact encouraged a mass influx of Jews from other parts of the country seeking to reestablish themselves in the capital.[14] After the Turkish defeat in World War I and the collapse of the Ottoman Empire, the Greeks occupied much of Turkey proper (1918-1922). Under Greek rule the Jews suffered from repeated outbreaks of anti-Semitism. Finally, the Treaty of Lausanne in 1923 established the present borders of Turkey. After the treaty, large communities, such as Istanbul, Adrianople, and Izmir were returned to Turkish rule.[15]

Throughout the period of Greek rule, the Jews of Turkey remained loyal to the Turks. However, they did not become integrated into Turkish society. In the larger cities, there were separate Jewish neighborhoods, Jewish children were usually educated either in Christian or Jewish schools, adult Jews shied away from Turkish politics, and until 1923, very few Turkish Jews could read or write Turkish, although many could speak it well.[16]

With international recognition of the new Turkish state granted under the Treaty of Lausanne on July 24, 1923, Turkey became a republic under the leadership of Kemal Ataturk, who had led the postwar revolution. Under the Treaty of Lausanne, the Turkish government was forced to recognize the rights of religious and ethnic minorities (par.39), who were permitted to have

132

their own social institutions, funds, and schools (par. 40). The Turkish government assured the minorities of their personal status as provided by the individual laws (par. 41).[17]

Although the treaty did little to better the condition of the Jews, other than now permitting them to use Hebrew as the language of instruction past the fourth grade in their schools, it did recognize Turkish Jewry as a protected minority. The Turkish revolutionary leadership regarded this status as subversive and dangerous, and as constituting a threat to the country's efforts at political and social integration. Fearing the consequences of hostile feelings, young Turkish Jewish intellectuals began intensive propaganda campaigns, to influence the community to reject minority status. Moreover, pressure was applied by the government in the form of propaganda campaigns, decrying the Jews as Spanish nationals. Under the combined pressures, the Jewish community, in a document of February 16, 1926, renounced minority status and affirmed the Jews' desire to live as full Turkish citizens. Subsequently the Greek and Armenian minorities were forced to follow the precedent set by the Jews.[18]

Renunciation of minority status meant the abolition of the Jews' special representation in the Turkish Parliament and their subjection to the full secularizing processes of the revolutionary regime. Turkish Jewry faced many restrictions under the regime of Ataturk, the most important being the gradual ousting of Jews from civil service positions and imposition of discriminatory restrictions on Jews in trade. In addition to specific anti-Jewish acts, the Jewish community of Turkey, like the rest of the population, was subjected to a series of laws designed to make Turkey a secular state. Religious marriages were banned, although Jews were permitted to have a religious ceremony if married first under civil law.

The teaching of Hebrew or other religious instruction in Jewish schools were banned. Clergy of all faiths were forbidden to grow beards or wear special garb; synagogues were closed and governmental support was taken away from Jewish schools. Until 1945 Jewish soldiers were denied officer status.[19]

The Jews of Thrace (European Turkey) suffered a worse fate. In July, 1934, Moslem masses pillaged Jewish homes and shops, and within a few days, 3,000 out of 13,000 Jews fled to Istanbul. These were the worst anti-Semitic attacks the Jews of Turkey had experienced in over a hundred years.[20]

The Turkish government policy was not fundamentally hostile to the Jews as such, but anti-foreign and anti-traditional. Thus, with the rise of Nazism, permission was granted Jews of non-Turkish nationality living in Turkey to remain and even to bring their families into the country to join them.[21] On the other hand, to meet the country's financial needs during World War II the neutral Turkish government approved a capital tax (varlik vergisi) in 1942. The determinants of a taxpayer's assessments were his religion and nationality. While the tax for Moslems and foreign citizens was 5 percent of their income or capital, non-Moslem inhabitants were forced to pay assessments made by special commissions, in accordance with the commissions' opinions. As a result, poor artisans and low wage-earners were left destitute and even the rich were bankrupted due to their inability to liquify their capital immediately.[22] In the spring and summer of 1943, the situation of the Jews worsened still, when the government began deporting non-Moslems, the majority of whom were Jews. However, by 1944, with the decline of German power, the capital tax was cancelled and defaulters were released from prison. Had the Jews not renounced their majority status in 1923, their capital tax assessments would most likely have been set at the same rate as that of

134

the Moslems'.   As it was, the cruelty and discrimination of the tax had a detrimental psychological effect
on the Jewish community and was one of the causes of
the mass emigration to Israel a few years later.[23] It
must be noted, however, that during the war the government took a tolerant and even helpful attitude
toward its Jewish citizens and foreign Jews as well,
allowing the Jewish Agency to operate in Turkey, together with the local Jewish community, to aid in the
illegal immigration of European Jewish refugees to
Palestine by way of Turkey.

The Democratic Party ruled in Turkey between 1950
and 1960.   During that period, restrictions on the
administration of the Jewish community were eased in
return for the Jewish vote. Synagogues formerly
closed were reopened and permission was granted for
new ones to be built.   Hebrew was permitted to be
included in the curriculum of the Jewish schools.   In
1960, a series of military juntas took over the
country and the revolution's original anti-religious
interpretation of the separation of church and state
once again became a basic principle in the government's platform.   A new constitution was written and
approved by popular referendum on July 9, 1961.   The
document contains guarantees on all basic human rights
and prohibits distinctions in law on the basis of
language, race, religion or personal convictions. In
its desire to have exclusive control over various
facets of the Turkish community, the new government
has since enforced the separation of religious and
secular administrative councils within the country and
at times has intervened in elections for the Jewish
council of Istanbul.

In the 1969 elections, for the first time since
1935, no Jew was elected to Parliament.[24]

There is little available statistical information
about the contemporary Turkish Jewish population. The

first population census of the Republic of Turkey was taken in 1926 and has been repeated at ten and, more recently, five year intervals. Later figures have been collected by the Jewish Agency and the World Jewish Congress based on evaluations made by community leaders, professional workers (Jewish Agency shlichim and Israeli Consulate staff) and visitors.

Official estimates of the size of the Jewish population in 1968, derived from 1965-1966 national census figures and estimates by various Jewish officials, suggest that there are between 35,000 and 40,000 Jews in the country, or approximately 0.1 percent of the total Turkish population.[25] Jewish Agency figures for 1970 total roughly 40,000 (see Table 5-1, p. 137). Unofficial estimates, however, are considerably lower. Cohen lists the Jews as 0.3 percent of the Turkish population and 2-3 percent of the population of Istanbul.[26]

A Turkish law grants special government recognition to religious communities of more than 15,000 members. The heads of such religious communities are granted many of the privileges given to diplomats, i.e., a car and chauffeur, a special flag, a special salary, etc. The head of the religious community is the official spokesman for the whole community and represents it to the government. In the period since government recognition was awarded the various groups, the Jewish population has dropped from more than 80,000 members to 40,000 or fewer, a number beginning to approach the minimum required for state recognition under law, and thus perhaps endangering the future legal status of the Jewish community.

The Jews are also afraid that even with their present numbers, the Moslem populace might conclude that the community should not continue to enjoy serious consideration or even its right to recognition.

Table 5-1

Distribution of the Jewish Population of Turkey

City	1927 Official Census	1965[a] Chief Rabbinate Estimates	1970[b] Jewish Institute Estimates
Adana	159	60	70
Ankara	633	800	3,200
Antaka (Antioch)	---	100	6
Bursa (Brusa)	1,915	350	400
Canakkale	---	420	300
Coclu	592	40	20
Dardanelles	1,109	---	---
Edirne (Adrianople)	6,098	400	120-400
Gallipoli	736	200	200
Gaziantep	742	160	---
Iskenderun	---	60	60
Istanbul	47,035	35,000	30,000
Izmir (Smyrna)	17,094	5,000	4,000-4,800
Kirklareli	978	90	35-67
Mersin	122	90	50
Milas	259	---	79
Tekirdag (Rodosto)	889	170	120
Tire	1,063	---	100
TOTAL	79,424	42,940	40,000

[a]According to letter, August 3, 1965.
[b]The institutions are the World Jewish Congress and the Jewish Agency.
SOURCE: Encyclopedia Judaica, vol. 15, p. 1459.

Not only might the external display of status be removed, but the community itself would face the potential anti-Jewish leanings of the Moslem majority, now kept more or less in balance. The Jewish community is the third largest minority in Turkey, following the Greeks and Armenians.

Over 95 percent of the Turkish Jewish population today is Sephardic.[27] Historically the Jews in Turkey formed three groups: a) those who had lived in the Byzantine Empire and came under Turkish rule after the fall of Byzantine; b) Sephardim exiled from Spain and Portugal; and c) Ashkenazim, who first came from Poland in the seventeenth and eighteenth centuries.[28] Later, there was also some immigration of Ashkenazim from Austria.[29] During the period of Nazi persecution, Turkey admitted many European Jews, especially those who had family in Turkey, and German and Austrian professors.[30] Since the end of World War II, except for Turkish Jews who emigrated to Israel and then returned to Turkey, there has been no significant Jewish immigration.[31]

Another part of the Turkish Jewish population is the Karaite community, originally an offshoot of Byzantine Jewry. About two hundred Karaite families (about 1,000 persons) live in the Hasköy section of Istanbul. Their only link to the Rabbinic community is the Rabbinate mohel, who performs their circumcisions.[32]

Since World War II the number of Jewish females in Turkey has exceeded that of Jewish males. The difference, however, seems to now be diminishing. A possible explanation for the predominance of women is that quite often males would emigrate first to Israel and prepare for their spouses to join them later.[33] Due to the lack of data, it is difficult to estimate the rates of births and deaths in the Jewish communities.[34]

138

The Jewish population in Turkey is concentrated in a few urban centers. There are two reasons for this phenomenon. First, the Jews have gravitated to the country's commercial centers as part of the overall trend towards urbanization and metropolitanization in Turkey and the world. Second, the majority of those who left Turkey were from the smaller communities. It is estimated that today approximately 84 percent of the entire Turkish community lives in Istanbul, while in 1927 only 51 percent resided there and in 1904 less than 45 percent.[35]

In Istanbul, there is a large migration out to the suburbs, resulting in a breakdown of organized Jewish synagogue affiliations (the main means of identification and affiliation). The government permits the maintenance of existing religious institutions but forbids the building of new ones. An exception was made in 1951, when the government granted permission to construct a synagogue on Heybeli Ada, one of the islands near Istanbul. Permission was granted in that case because one of the influential members of the Jewish community, Solomon Adato, was also a Member of Parliament and was able to influence the government to grant the charter. Another island, Buyukada, also has a new synagogue, but it has only a temporary permit.

The sections of Istanbul that have the largest concentrations of Jews are: Beyoglu, Kasimpassa, Sisli, Hasköy, Balat, Ortaköy, Kuzzauuck, Kadiköy (Haydar Pacha), Sireci, Galata, Tunel, Taksim, Nisantas, and Macka.[36] In addition there are large summer communities on three of the islands that divide the city, the largest communities being located on Buyukada and Heybeli Ada. A motivating force in suburbanization is the increasing prosperity of Istanbul Jewry and the accompanying desire for more opulent homes in more exclusive neighborhoods.[37]

At the end of the nineteenth century, largely due to economic conditions, Jews began to emigrate from Turkey in substantial numbers, mostly to Egypt, the Americas, and in a small way to Israel. Since World War I the thrust of this emigration has been in the direction of Israel.[38] Immediately after the establishment of the State of Israel, that flow increased so greatly as to radically change the face of the community remaining in Turkey. In 1948, a total of 4,362 Jews emigrated to Israel. Emigration was forbidden from November 1948 until early 1949, as a result of pressure upon the Turkish government by the various Arab states, but once Turkey recognized the State of Israel "de jure" in 1949, the government lifted its restrictions and even aided emigrants by putting ships at their disposal. In 1950, Israeli representatives were allowed to operate in Turkey to organize emigration procedures.

The first large wave of Turkish Jewish immigrants to Israel were from the working class, or those people who were welfare cases. In recent years, definitely since 1967 but perhaps even before, immigrants have been quite well-to-do, many of them professionals. During 1949-1950, a total of 26,295 Jews emigrated to Israel. The number fell after 1950, when the economic situation in Turkey improved, although the only governmental restriction on emigrants was that they were forbidden to take property out with them.[39]

It is estimated that from 1948 to 1956, approximately 37,538 Jews emigrated to Israel, of whom some 3,000 to 3,500 eventually returned to Turkey.[40] Emigration increased in the latter part of the 1950's, as a result of anti-minorities riots (1956), but slowed down again in the 1960's.[41] Since the Six Day War some 2,000 to 3,000 Jews have emigrated to Israel from Turkey, approximately 1,500 of whom came in the last two years.[42] Official Israel government statistics on Turkish immigration are available only through

1964; Jewish Agency statistics are available for 1972 and 1973.[43] One Jewish Agency official claims that since the establishment of the State of Israel, 80,000 Jews have emigrated to it from Turkey;[44] this estimate, however, seems considerably inflated.

In addition to immigration to Israel, a steady, although small, percentage of Jews has continued to emigrate westward to North and South America. Furthermore, many young Turkish Jews study in French and Austrian universities, eventually settling in those lands.[45] One authority estimates that in the period from 1948 to 1973 as many as 20,000 Jews have emigrated to countries other than Israel.[46]

Aside from economic factors encouraging emigration since World War I, political considerations have also been apparent. For instance, many Jews left Izmir in the Greco-Turkish War. During the 1930's many more Jews were forced to leave the European part of Turkey, and still more left the country in and following 1942, as a result of the enormous property tax. Again in the late 1950's, when Jewish property was threatened, the Jews felt how little they were accepted by the majority of Turks.[47] However, unless there is another major act committed against the Jews, those who today remain in Turkey will probably continue to live there, even if, as the trend shows, Jewish life continues to decline.

Initially, the economic status of Turkish Jewry benefitted by the Turkish revolution, as the Jews moved into the places previously held by the Greeks and Armenians in trade, especially after the Greek exodus of 1922. The number of Jewish academics and clerks, many of whom were attached to Turkish banks and big mercantile companies, also increased. Competence in the Turkish language, which the Jews were now making every effort to learn, facilitated their advancement. Thus, the Jewish communities of Istanbul

141

and Izmir passed through a period of relative economic growth from 1922 until 1942, when the Property Tax was enacted. As a consequence of the tax most Jews went bankrupt and were forced into menial labor or were put into prisons.[49]

Today Jews in Turkey are active in almost all spheres of the Turkish economy. Studies showed that, in 1966, 96 percent of the available Jewish work force was gainfully employed and that about ten percent of that work force was composed of women. The majority of the Jews either held administrative or managerial positions (approximately 5,000) or were salesmen and merchants (5,100). Another 1,000 were skilled or semi-skilled workers in textile, electrical, communications and other industries. Among the 700 craftsmen listed were tailors, furriers, shoemakers, etc., while another 600 people were employed as domestics and in related jobs. There were 575 Jews engaged in the professions and arts, including medicine, architecture, education, law, music, literature and the fine arts.[50] Table 5-2 (page 143) gives a statistical breakdown of occupations.[51] The percentage of Jewish working women is somewhat higher than the national average, especially in the secretarial and clerical fields.[52]

Generally, one can assume that the economic position of the Jewish community in Turkey today is fairly good; indeed, it is considerably better than it was in the 1940's.[53] There are very few poor Jews in Turkey today, most having emigrated to Israel after the establishment of the state, and those remaining Jews who are in need are not an undue financial burden on the community. Social service benefits are good, and retired Jews can usually live comfortably on their pensions. Were such people to emigrate to Israel, they would lose all these rights.

In general, the Jewish population is more literate than the general population. According to

Table 5-2

Occupations of Jews in Turkey Aged 15 and Over (1960)

Occupation	Percentage
Free Professions and Technical Work	6.0
Administration	35.0
Trade	33.0
Artisans	15.7
Manual Labor	2.3
Transportation	1.1
Services	5.5
Agriculture	1.1
Fishing and Quarrying	.02
TOTAL	99.72
Wage-earners whose occupations are known	14,527

SOURCE: Turkey, Census of Population, 1960.
Quoted in Cohen, Hayyim, Hayehudim
B'Artzot HaMizrach Hatichon B'Yamenu,
Hebrew University Press, 1972, Table B-3,
p. 97.

the 1965 census, only 10 percent of the entire Jewish population was illiterate, as compared with more than one-third of the general population. Ladino used to be the "native tongue" of Turkish Jewry, with French used among the more westernized elements. Data from the 1960 and 1965 census reports show that the use of Ladino has declined. In 1960 it was named as their mother-tongue by 19,000 Jews, almost all living in large cities, and an additional 4,300 said that although Turkish was their mother-tongue, Ladino was their second language. By 1965 the figures had dropped by 30 to 50 percent, with only 8,000 to 10,000 claiming Ladino as their mother-tongue.[54]

The 1960 census listed one hundred Jews as speaking Yahudice in the far-eastern city of Van. These people were probably remnants of a Turkish-speaking Jewish community which disappeared in the early 1960's, as a result of emigration to Israel.

Other languages used by members of the Jewish community, according to the 1965 census, were German and Slavic languages, used mainly in the Istanbul Ashkenazi community, and English, French, and Italian. These latter languages are often the languages of instruction of the foreign schools where many Turkish children study.[55]

According to the Chief Rabbi of Turkey, the rate of intermarriage with non-Jewish spouses of both sexes has been steadily increasing since the decade of the 1960's. Some of the older population see this as a serious threat to the continued existence of the community.[56] The rate of assimilation has also increased within the last ten years. One of the contributing factors in this trend is the increase in the rate of higher education of both Turkish and Jewish youth, since the university gives them a common meeting place. Until recently there was not much interest on the part of Jews in mingling with the

Turkish community, the Jews seeing themselves as being more cultured and educated than their Turkish Moslem counterparts. It is feared that with the gaps in education closing, young Jews are encouraged to seek friendships outside their community.

Jews, like other minorities, are protected under the Turkish Constitution.[57] Nevertheless, there are certain problems which they face.

Anti-Semitism in Turkey can be classified under four separate, if overlapping, headings: (1) government aggression against Jews as part of its aggression against all minority and foreign groups within Turkey; (2) enactments against Jewish religion and education, as part of the government's emphasis on the secularization of life; (3) overt anti-Semitic acts as a result of the higher economic standard of the Jewish community; and (4) anti-Israel-oriented acts.

There is little or no official anti-Semitism in Turkey today. As reported elsewhere, Jews no longer pay special taxes, nor are they treated differently from other citizens in the eyes of the law or with regard to military service. Although the Jews are a small group within a large Moslem majority, they are subjected to no particular harassment because of their Judaism.

Anti-Semitism in the press is a periodic problem. In 1948, articles appeared in the Turkish press denouncing Jewish emigration to Israel on the grounds that it would undermine the Turkish economy and that Communists were among the organizers of the exodus.[58] In 1955 and 1956 anti-Semitic press articles appeared frequently in Turkish newspapers. At the urging of the Jewish community, the government cracked down on these papers, although the most notorious of the writers, Refat Atilhan, continued publishing until his death in 1961.[59] The blatantly anti-Semitic

145

newspaper, Büyük Dogu, published many harsh attacks between 1951 and 1961.[60]

During the 1969 election campaign, anti-Semitic propaganda was circulated by rightist groups, which arose as a product of the more tolerant government attitude toward Moslem religious activities at the time. Propaganda attacks consisted of accusing the Jews of exploiting the nation's economy, of deception and black-marketeering. Finally, the government closed down the Bügün, the right-wing Istanbul daily newspaper printing these attacks, and the editor was forced to flee the country to avoid arrest.[61]

It is known that Turkish nationals have trained in El Fatah camps in Syria.[62] In 1969 and again in 1972 and 1973, Palestinian or Arab terrorists acted in Turkey. In 1969 a Jordanian student was killed and another wounded when a bomb they intended to plant at the Israel Pavilion of the Izmir International Fair exploded in their car. In 1972, Israeli Consul Yigal Alrom was shot down in Istanbul,[63] and in 1973 terrorist bombs damaged the Israel Pavilion of the Fair in Izmir.

Turkish citizens are permitted no international affiliations. In terms of Jewish communal life this means that Zionist organizations and fund-raising and international Jewish organizations, like B'nai Brith and the World Jewish Congress, are forbidden. Activities with an international flavor exist within the community, clandestinely, and the Jews live in constant fear of these activities being exposed. Organizations are given different names, meetings are closed to the public, and no membership cards, certificates, or other symbols are distributed. Israel-oriented programs are not advertised as such, and care is taken to have other entertainment available in case of a raid.

146

In the 1955 anti-minorities riots and, to a lesser extent, in the 1964 anti-Greek riots, Jewish shops were destroyed, while the government did little to prevent rioters from accomplishing their aims. When, in 1964, Turkey forbade Greek citizens from living, working, or holding property in Turkey, twenty-four Jews were expelled, although as Greek nationals of non-Greek origin they should have been exempt from exile and confiscation. Many of the remaining 336 Greek Jews emigrated, while the rest applied for Turkish citizenship.[64]

Since the days of Ataturk, the government has tried to repress religious, especially Moslem activities in the country. Many of these measures have already been described. The Jewish community must face such problems daily. The Turkish Foundations Administration, or Vakif, supervises the expenditures and income of all congregations and allows only minimal repairs on religious and communal structures. If requests are presented for more extensive repairs, the community must wait long periods of time for an answer.

In 1972, fourteen people who had been members of Turkey's Central Jewish Communal Council in 1966-1967 were arrested for "negligence of duty." The Vakif charged that in 1967, the communal council "misused its powers by spending more than the minimal limit of funds, without approval, on repairs and other work done on Jewish Community properties in downtown Istanbul." The Central Communal Council was asked to explain where the money had come from, as it was a great deal more than appeared on the budget submitted to the Vakif. It was explained that the money had been contributed or loaned by one of the members of this community, who had since emigrated. Although charges were dropped against the defendants, the member who was said to have "contributed" the money has not been allowed to return to Turkey.

Another recent trial also concerned several members of the Istanbul Jewish community. In 1973, a group of teachers was arrested for "illegally" teaching Hebrew and Jewish subjects. Under Turkish law, only teachers certified by the state are permitted to teach religion. In Machazike Torah, a religious educational institution chartered by the state, older students and "graduates" of Machazike Torah teach the younger children, while rabbis teach the older ones. A Moslem teacher at the Jewish Day School informed the police that the Jews were teaching illegally. The teachers were arrested and trial procedures initiated against them. It is assumed that the charges will be quietly dropped, but both cases are good examples of existing restrictions on Jewish life.

These restrictions are by-products of Turkish suspicion of Greek, and to a lesser extent, Armenian nationalist activity. They also reflect the government's desire to minimize religious life in Turkey. If Jews were allowed to open new schools where religion was taught, permission would have to be granted to the Moslems and to the other minorities, who are constantly battling the government on this issue. The government was probably well aware that some of the teachers in Machazike Torah had no formal training, but accepted this system as long as no conflict arose. However, when the Moslem teacher, representing her religious faction, which also wants its own schools and classes, issued a complaint, the government was forced to act. By the same token, if Jewish communal activities were not restricted, the government could not restrict the activities of the Greek community, of which it has been so suspicious for so long. In general, the Jews have been able to circumvent many of the restrictions on communal life by paying bribes, carrying on clandestine activities, falsifying reports, and establishing new congregations on temporary permits.

In summary, although there is little or no anti-Semitism per se today and although the Jews are protected under the Turkish constitution, the Jewish community lives in fear of anti-Semitic acts occurring in the future. This, among other things, explains why the community is not active politically or communally and why it is so afraid of publicity. This fear can be seen in the local Jews' hesitation to invite Israeli officials to their homes, their efforts to speak Turkish in public, their fear of publicizing Jewish population statistics, and the like.

Most non-Jews in Turkey do not concern themselves with Jewish life and the problems of the Jewish community. The general media conveys relatively objective information on Israel, both from Lebanese and Western sources.[65] The Eichmann case was reported in the Turkish papers and whatever interest there was proved favorable to the Jews. However, most Turks did not show an interest in the trial.[66] The Jews and the Jewish community do not seem to play any part in shaping non-Jewish treatment of Jewish issues.

Since the 1960 coup established the Committee of National Unity, it has always taken pains to be represented at important minority functions (the funeral of Chief Rabbi Saban, official visits to the synagogue on Yom Kippur, etc.).[67]

The Structure of the Turkish Jewish Community

Pre-modern Turkey was organized on the basis of the millet system. That is to say, every non-Moslem minority was granted a substantial measure of internal self-rule within the Ottoman Empire, and the appropriate communal institutions existed to maintain

149

internal control on behalf of the Sultan. Thus the Jewish community could follow its own laws on many matters and administer its own affairs within the limits imposed by the Ottoman authorities.

Even after Turkish rule was consolidated in 1453, the Jews continued the organizational patterns they had developed during the Byzantine period. When the Spanish Jews arrived, an organization called the Kiahyalik, headed by the Chief Rabbi, was established, which represented the community to the government. However, friction soon developed between the Spanish Jewish community and the older Jewish elements, causing a division into two separate bodies, each having its own Chief Rabbi. The Sephardim further fragmented into small groups, based on their cities of origin on the Iberian Peninsula. As a consequence, the office of the Chief Rabbi of Turkey was discontinued for a period of over two hundred years, until its reestablishment in 1936.[68]

When the two communities were merged, at the demand of the Sultan, the new community acquired an administrative structure similar to the one in current operation. Under this organizational structure, each synagogue was autonomous and was administered by appointees who dealt with the collection of taxes and managed congregational affairs. All synagogues came under the control of the High Rabbinical Court.[69] In addition to the synagogue administration there was a general council of the whole community, headed by the Chief Rabbi, with two divisions: a Religious Council of seven rabbis and a Bet Din, and a secular council, composed of notables of the community.

The "Statut Organique" of the Jewish Community of Istanbul, approved by Sultan Abdul Aziz in 1864, formulated the status of the Jewish community and its administration according to the millet principle but along western legal lines, fixing the number of

150

council members at nine.[70] A later statute set the number of council members at twenty religious and sixty secular members. Later, seven rabbis were elected as a religious council and nine secular members as a secular council.[71] Still another statute of the Istanbul Jewish community, adopted in 1914, defined the situation of rabbis, classifying them into four categories.[72] The Rabbinical Court was composed of from three to five members.

That was the situation before the conclusion of the Turkish revolution in 1923. One of the principal goals of the revolution was the abolition of the millet system and the transformation of Turkey into a modern, secular nation-state, essentially homogenous in population and certainly under a single, secular law. Kemal Ataturk's doctrine, which has been applied more or less strictly since the revolution, is that any minority community activities determined by the authorities to be secular in character are to be exclusively a function of the state.[73] All minority groups were thus officially informed that their community organizations were henceforth limited to religious matters.

Until 1949, centralized community organizations were tolerated but not recognized. In 1950, a new law concerning endowments required that each property devoted to religious purposes must be managed independently by a committee chosen by the congregants. Another law concerning associations dictated that each individual charity must be organized as an independent association.[74] The new constitution and a decree in 1961 outlawed the council of non-rabbinical leaders for a time, but it is now once more permitted to function, although without official government recognition.[75]

The only legally recognized countrywide Jewish community structure today is the Chief Rabbinate.

151

However, although the Chief Rabbinate maintains liaison with communities throughout the country and represents them in all official business with the government, it is actually able to control the activities of only the Istanbul community.[76] Its influence in other communities is, however, strong. Between the years 1931 and 1953 there was no Chief Rabbi, the community having failed to replace the previous incumbent, who had died. As a result, the spiritual, communal, and educational life of the community deteriorated.

Since 1953 there have been two Chief Rabbis: Raphael Saban and David Asseo. Today, some forty full-time employees administer the foundations, or Vakifs of the Chief Rabbinate in Istanbul.[77] The Chief Rabbi appoints a Religious Council, consisting of a Rosh Bet Din (mara de atra) and four Hahamim.[78] The Haham Basilik (Chief Rabbinate) and the Religious Council have supervision over marriages, divorces, deaths, births, kashrut, and, apparently, education. The Bet Din hears civil arbitration cases but only rarely, since it does not have sufficient status in the eyes of most of the community to encourage utilization of its facilities beyond what Turkish law requires.

Istanbul today is divided into Jewish districts, known as Hashgahot. Each of these (or, in one case, a combination of several) districts has a synagogue, the administration of which is carried out by a vaad hakehilla (communal council), approved under the 1950 law mentioned above. There are ten communal councils: Galata-Sisli; Buyukada; Kadikoy-Gida Bustan; Balat; Hasköy; Kazzauuck; Ortaköy; Sireci; the Ashkenazi community; and the Italian community. Each council is composed of from four to seven members, depending on the size of the congregation. In accordance with the laws mentioned above, each synagogue is legally autonomous and is directly responsible to a government foundation, <u>Vakif</u>, to which the synagogue council must submit a yearly financial report in which it states the income and expenditures of the congregation. These reports do not reflect the true financial status of the congregations, which, while forbidden under law, do, in fact, have a unified communal adminis- tration. The largest district communal council is the one combining the districts of Beyoglu, Kasimpassa, and Sisli in Congregation Neve Shalom, which has approximately 10,000 members. It is believed that in addition to the separate district communal councils, there exists a <u>Vaad</u> <u>Hakelali</u>, or <u>Conseil</u> <u>Communal</u>, which is a central council.

The umbrella organization of secular communal life is the <u>Conseil</u> <u>Laique</u>, which has about thirty members, seven or eight of whom are active. Its fund- raising arm is the "Coordination." The various charitable and communal organizations and institutions submit their budget requests to the "Coordination," which provides them with their operating funds. The Chief Rabbi appoints five members to the <u>Conseil</u> <u>Laique</u> probably representing various institutions, and the district councils appoint the other members.

The interrelationship between the Religious Council and the <u>Conseil</u> <u>Laique</u> is very strong. The <u>Conseil</u> <u>Laique</u> represents the various facets of the community and manages all the community's affairs, as it is unlawful for the Rabbinate to deal with finances. It advises the Chief Rabbi in many fields and really serves as an all-embracing communal organization. But because it cannot work openly, it is dependent on the Chief Rabbinate to be its spokesman and representative to the government.

Until 1850 there was no community where Jews lived that did not have at least one <u>heder</u>. In 1889 approximately 2,500 children in Istanbul alone were receiving a <u>Talmud</u> <u>Torah</u> education in twenty-eight different schools. The first modern Hebrew Day School was founded in 1850 and by 1868 the Alliance Israelite Universelle had begun operating. In 1902, one of the large Talmudei Torah merged with one of the Alliance schools in Istanbul and in subsequent years Talmudei Torah in Adrianople and Izmir also merged with Alliance schools. As a consequence of the shift toward a more secular education, the number of students studying in institutions of higher Jewish education (yeshivot) diminished,[79] so that, whereas in the nineteenth century Turkey had been renowned for its Jewish scholarship, by the 1960's the one remaining yeshiva--the Rabbinical Seminary--closed down for lack of students.[80]

The last seminary in Turkey had first opened in Adrianople in 1892, introducing into its curriculum courses in Jewish philosophy and literature, after the Sephardic fashion. Moving to Istanbul in 1895, the seminary remained open until World War II. After the war, it reopened for a short time. In 1955, under the financial and advisory sponsorship of the Jewish Agency, it opened once again and at its peak had several hundred students. When enrollment began to drop again, a program was instituted where students were accepted after only five years of schooling, with the ensuing course of studies lasting seven years. The Turkish government recognized the seminary as a religious vocational school, but did not allow graduates to sit for university matriculation examinations.[81] This was probably an influential factor in the continued decline in enrollment, until finally the seminary closed down again in the late 1960's.

Turkish law allows children of minorities to study in government schools. In addition, Jewish children also study in foreign schools. Although the Treaty of Lausanne permitted the minorities to use foreign languages as the language of instruction in their schools, the Jews relinquished this right along

154

with other rights when they opted for full Turkish citizenship. As a result, by 1928, all Alliance schools, where the language of instruction was French, had either closed down or were transferred to the administration of the communities, and Turkish was the only language used. In 1945 the government permitted the introduction of Hebrew and religion into the curriculum on a limited scale (four hours a week); otherwise the curriculum remained the standard one issued by the Ministry of Education.[82] The teachers must be certified by the Ministry of Education, after having taken university or pedagogical courses.

Today all the Jewish schools in Istanbul are combined into the Istanbul Jewish School, comprising classes from grades one through eleven. The school is divided into three sections: an elementary school for the first five years of study, a three year junior high school, and a three year secondary school, the Lycee B'nai Brith, which was founded in 1915. Students pay a tuition fee, with the community subsidizing the school to cover the fees of the needy. At one time the educational and social levels of the school were very high, but the standards have dropped considerably in recent years.

The elementary school division has an all-Jewish student body. The schools are registered under Turkish law as Turkish Jewish schools, thus excluding children of other nationalities and religions. In the junior high and high school divisions over 90 percent of the children are Jewish and the rest are Moslem. However, in the elementary schools, more than 80 percent of the teachers are Moslem and, in the junior high and high school, there are only two Jewish teachers; all the rest are Moslems, including both the principal and assistant principal.

Tuition at the First Jewish Elementary School (<u>Musevi Birinji Karma</u>) is free, in order to attract

155

students who would otherwise be unable to pay for their studies, and in the Second Jewish Elementary School it is TL 40 per month. In the junior high and secondary school divisions fees are TL 100. It should be noted that all education in Turkish government-sponsored schools is free, including secondary school, while the tuition costs at most foreign schools, especially French, are from TL 3000 to 5000 per year. About 30 percent of the students attending Jewish schools receive subsidies from the Jewish community for their tuition fees, and another 10 percent of the students win stipends given by the School Board.

The students in all Jewish schools receive five hours of Hebrew instruction a week, taught by the community rabbis. There are no formal Judaica classes, but short discussions and explanations about Judaism are given during Hebrew classes.

At one time the educational and social levels of the school were very high, but the standards have dropped considerably in recent years, and children who plan to attend university or children of wealthier parents usually attend the foreign (mostly English, French, or American) schools or government schools.

Within the last ten years the enrollment in the Jewish school has dropped tremendously.[83] It is possible to explain part of the decrease in enrollment by again citing the fact that the old, established Jewish neighborhoods are breaking up, as wealthy Jews move to the various suburbs. In addition, it is felt by some that leaders in the community do not recognize the need to maintain and upgrade Jewish day school education, and that by sending their own children to foreign schools, as most of the wealthy Jews do, they are perpetuating the image of the Jewish schools as second-rate institutions.

The only other Jewish Day School functioning in Turkey today is to be found in Izmir. Founded as a communal high school in 1915, it later became an elementary school for grades one through five.[84] In 1958 another attempt was made to open a Jewish secondary school, but it closed down in 1971. There were (and perhaps still are) students from Izmir who study at the Musevi Lisesi (Lycee B'nai Brith) in Istanbul. There is some adult Jewish education in Izmir, centering around the synagogue.[85]

The other institution that concerns itself with providing a traditional Jewish education is Machazike Torah, founded about thirty-five years ago by Rabbi Nisim Behar and now affiliated with the Rabbinates of Istanbul and Izmir. Machazike Torah has a government permit to carry on its religious education activities, which consist of Talmud Torah classes held on Shabbat and Sunday, where prayers and Judaica are taught, Shabbat and holiday services and social activities. It is estimated that about 2,000 youth, ranging from six through sixteen years of age, receive religious instruction through Machazike Torah in Istanbul and Izmir. In this way, approximately fifty percent of the Jewish children in Turkey receive some kind of Jewish education.

In addition to classes for children, Machazike Torah also trains religious functionaries, such as hazzanim, shochatim and mohalim. Classes in Machazike Torah are led by graduates of the system and in addition there are three young native rabbis, also graduates of Machazike Torah, who, after receiving their rabbinical training in Israel, returned to serve as community rabbis. Machazike Torah is financially supported by the Istanbul Jewish community, but its income does not always cover its expenses. It is not known whether the Jewish Agency also gives financial assistance. (The recent trial involving Machazike

157

Torah teachers has been discussed in the section dealing with anti-Semitism.)

There are six Jewish clubs in Turkey, five of them in the Istanbul area and the other in Izmir. There is no organized Jewish social or cultural life in other Jewish communities, except for activities that center around the synagogue, and then only at special times, such as religious holidays or special occasions, such as bar mitzvahs, weddings, and the like.

The Youth, Sport and Social clubs sponsored by the Jewish community in Istanbul are: Dostluk, Yildirim Spor, Amical, Kardeslik, Or Hahayim, and Machazike Torah. Each group has a charter granted by the government, which entitles it to operate under Turkish law either as a social or sport club. The common language used in the clubs is Turkish. In order to serve both financial and cultural goals, the clubs prepare special events, such as plays and folklore nights to which adults are invited, as well as purely social evenings for the youngsters. Most clubhouses contain a discotheque, library and sports facilities. Dostluk also has a kosher restaurant. Meeting halls are provided in some cases in the synagogue or community centers. Although formally no different than any other Turkish clubs, these groups quietly sponsor programs dealing with Israel and Judaism. The Organization and Public Relations, Youth and Hechalutz, and Sephardic Communities departments of the Jewish Agency and the World Zionist Organization supply educational materials, lecturers and entertainers. Events have been held commemorating Holocaust Day and Independence Day, as well as classes in Israeli folk dancing, Bible, Jewish history, and Hebrew. (At its peak, Dostluk offered sixteen different Hebrew classes, taught by local teachers.)

158

Technically, all the clubs are interdenominational; however, none of them accepts non-Jewish members. A clause in the constitution of each club requires prospective members to be endorsed by existing members, thus ensuring control over the selection of newcomers. If members do bring non-Jews to activities, the members are requested by the management to leave, or at least not to bring such friends again.

The largest of the clubs, Dostluk (Friendship), was founded in 1966 by older members of the student body of Machazike Torah, who felt the need for a coeducational social club, where boys and girls could mingle socially more freely than at Machazike Torah. Substantial sums were contributed by individuals in the community and a very modern and well-equipped community center was built in the new section of Sisli. In 1971, Dostluk had 300 to 400 members, but it is thought that there has been a decline since then, perhaps because some of the leadership has emigrated to Israel.

Differing from other youth clubs, from its inception, Dostluk tried to encourage participation by adults as well as youth, attracting them with classes and cultural programs, as well as having adults sit on the board of directors, along with younger people. A folklore group, which performs only Israeli dances, is extremely active, and the discotheques on Saturday nights are also popular. Often such activities are incorporated into "Israeli nights," with Israeli food and music.

The original directorate of the club comprised all the initiators, but subsequent councils were composed of twelve members: four older members of the community, four young adults and four students. Currently the board has eight members, four adults and

159

four younger members. Elections are held annually, but they are pro forma.

The expenses of <u>Dostluk</u> were initially met through contributions, membership fees and tickets to events, paid by the adults (students are never asked to pay), but lately it has been necessary to accept a subsidy from the community, as fewer adults are active members. The facilities of <u>Dostluk</u> are rented out for weddings and bar mitzvahs, with the members themselves catering. Neither the membership nor the leadership of <u>Dostluk</u> think of themselves as representing the Establishment in the community; probably some of the contributors and board members do take part in community affairs, however.

<u>Yildirim</u> <u>Spor</u> is officially recognized as a sports club. In accordance with Turkish law, the club offers activities in five sports areas, but its level of achievement is not very high. Actually, the club is very active socially and often resembles the clubhouse of an Israeli youth organization. In the folk dance competition held in honor of Israel's twenty-fifth anniversary, the <u>Yildirim</u> folk dance group won the trophy, supplied from Israel.

<u>Amical</u> is a club catering mostly to students and high school graduates. Most of the club's activities are social, although geared to a sophisticated level. Unlike <u>Dostluk</u>, <u>Amical</u> is very much an Establishment organization, sponsored heavily by the community. It also has a folklore troupe and has hopes of winning the next folk dance trophy.

<u>Or</u> <u>haHayim</u> Club is an offshoot of a charity project conducted by community youngsters each year, in which pairs of youngsters are sent to collect money for the <u>Or</u> <u>haHayim</u> Hospital. The youth have banded together into a permanent club, which, since it has no

meeting place of its own, is aided by <u>Amical</u>. It also has a folklore troupe.

<u>Machazike</u> <u>Torah</u> activities have been described previously. Naturally, the leadership is interested in holding its youngsters together in social as well as educational activities for as long as possible.

<u>Kardeslik</u> Club differs from the other clubs in that it is principally for adults. Home studies in Hebrew are conducted by a local teacher. In addition, there is a women's group, parallel to an Israeli WIZO group, which is quite active socially, giving frequent teas and dinners. The group is aided by the Jewish Agency.

The only youth club in Izmir, <u>Kultur</u> <u>Gemiyeti</u>, conducts social activities for the community's youth. Recently, the club's drama group gave a successful performance of a play by Rostan and was due to give a three-night performance in Istanbul at the <u>Dostluk</u> Center.

Ideological identification of Turkish Jewish youth has fallen off in recent years. An indication of this trend is the shift in membership from ideological organizations, such as <u>Kadima</u> <u>Tziona</u> (which was founded in 1962 and reached its peak in 1967), to affiliation with more purely social groups.[86]

Religious life, which is the only real means of identification and involvement the average Jewish adult has with the organized Jewish community in Turkey, is now at a much lower ebb than in former years. In fact, it has reached a point where some community leaders, especially in Izmir, feel that there is a definite danger of the community disintegrating, at least from a religious point of view. The situation is most critical in the small communities,

161

where there are no religious functionaries of any kind, except for a handful of old men who have no formal qualifications but possess a great desire to continue the traditions. The Ashkenazi congregation in Istanbul is very small and must pay its members in order to maintain a minyan. The situation is better in the city's Sephardic synagogues, where most Jews attend services on the holidays. It is officially estimated that in 1967, approximately seventy-five synagogues were open in Turkey, about thirty-five of which were in actual use. It is reported that in Istanbul alone there are fifty synagogues, including ten to fifteen which hold services on the Sabbath and holidays. Some believe that these figures are exaggerated and that there are less than ten operative congregations. Synagogues also exist in Adana, Ankara, Bursa, Edirne (Adrianople), and Izmir, while smaller communities sometimes also hold services.[87] Synagogues are kept in excellent condition, even after being closed down for lack of worshippers who have moved to other centers or who emigrated. Maintenance costs are financed through individual contributions.

There is supervised ritual slaughtering in Turkey, but the number of people demanding kosher food is small. The Chief Rabbinate tries to supply shochatim to large centers and, in special circumstances, to outlying communities as well. However, there is a shortage of qualified shochatim who are willing to live in communities other than Istanbul. For instance, the Izmir community is interested in supporting a shochet ready to make the move. There are two Jewish butchers in Istanbul (who sell both kosher and non-kosher meat) and one Moslem butcher who also sells kosher meat.[88]

Except for the prohibition on building new synagogues, there have been no recent hindrances on the part of the Turkish authorities regarding religious observances. However, most of the younger

162

generation are not observant, and many young people are entirely ignorant of Judaism.[89] To counteract this trend, the Chief Rabbi introduced the bat-mitzvah ceremony and gave the bar-mitzvah ceremony more communal importance. In this connection, the Istanbul and Izmir communities have requested from the Jewish Agency such basic ritual articles as mezzuzot, kippot, tefillin and talitot, most of which were to be given as bar-mitzvah and bat-mitzvah gifts by the community.

Some of the community feel that neither the Chief Rabbinate nor the leaders of the communities have sufficiently provided for the continuance of religious life in succeeding generations. It is claimed that, in addition to their lack of stress on education for children, they have not done enough to encourage youth to study for the rabbinate or to become other communal functionaries.

Most of the fund-raising operations for local charities are carried out by members of the "Coordination," who have a list of all members of the Jewish community over the age of 18 and who make systematic annual appeals to each breadwinner, suggesting a sum of money the committee has previously decided upon, according to each contributor's economic situation.[90] This is in effect an informal voluntary communal tax. Another informal tax, called a kitzbah, finances the activities of the Chief Rabbinate and community religious services. It is estimated that two-thirds of the community's budget is raised through these taxes and other contributions. In addition, the Jewish community has property granted it in Ottoman times; income from these properties, held by the Haham Basilik Vakif (Foundation of the Chief Rabbinate), constitutes the remaining one-third.

Small fees are taken in from weddings, circumcisions, bar-mitzvahs and funerals, kosher meat, etc., as well as from the sale of synagogue seats in most of the synagogues for the High Holy Days.[91]

A large share of the community's finances are provided through the sale of mitzvot in the synagogue. The traditional social ritual developed centuries ago around the sale of these honors has been maintained. Many of the wealthy and influential people of the community attend synagogue services and vie for different honors--being called to the Torah, to open the ark, to light the Havdalah candle, etc. Individual donations to the synagogue, its functionaries and all the institutions and organizations are announced, and thus immediate public recognition is given for all contributions. Discussing the amount of money each person contributed serves as a popular topic of conversation for that week among all the members of the community. It also, incidentally, prolongs the religious service by hours, and, in opposition to such displays, the Machazike Torah congregation, Knesset Yisrael, does not permit the sale of mitzvot. The Chief Rabbi also tried to abolish the system in the late 1960's, but with little success.[92]

A variation of the mitzvot sales was used by the youngsters who founded Dostluk Center. Since the inaugural community meeting was held on Tu B'Shvat, they "sold" the brachot--various blessings said by the Sephardim on this holiday--and auctioned off Membership Card no. 1 of the club as well. About TL 25,000 was raised in this way. Furthermore, substantial contributors to the club were elected to the board of directors. It is assumed that similar fund-raising methods are used in other clubs.

Or-haHayim Hospital has a regular box-collection campaign, run with the help of the community's youngsters, as described previously, and is also heavily subsidized by the government.

164

Contributions to Israel are against the law, since it is illegal to take currency out of the country, and offenders are severely punished. However, some contributions do get to Israel, no doubt with the tacit consent of the authorities.

The Jewish press is represented in Istanbul by two independent Jewish weeklies: Salom, edited by Avram Leyon and Victor Apulaci, and La Vera Luz, edited by Eliezer Mende and Luna Horman. In both papers Ladino is used, written in Turkish orthography. There is some indication that La Vera Luz may have ceased publication recently. About 750-800 families subscribe to Salom throughout Turkey and the paper has limited circulation abroad (Czechoslovakia, Sweden, Denmark, Nicaragua, Italy, U.S.A.). In general Salom is an anti-Establishment publication and frequently attacks the Rabbinate and community leaders.

The Jewish elite subscribes to Le Journal d'Orient, owned by Albert Karasu, a member of the Istanbul Jewish community. Although the paper is a general Turkish newspaper published in French, it frequently contains articles of Jewish interest. The Chief Rabbinate issues bulletins of a religious nature (candle lighting times, summaries of Jewish law and Bible portions, etc.). Some of the youth clubs also have bulletins.[93] The Hebrew press closed down in 1944.

A wealth of material on the Turkish Jewish community throughout its history is available in the archives of the Chief Rabbinate. At present, it lies untapped as a scholarly resource.[94]

Political Dynamics of the Turkish Jewish Community

In discussing the system of voluntary leadership of the Istanbul community, the dominant position held by the Society for the Support of the Poor must be stressed. Under other circumstances this society would have been a B'nai Brith Lodge. Because B'nai Brith has been banned in Turkey since the Revolution, many of its former members and those who have followed in their footsteps have chosen this means to carry on many of their fraternal relationships. The Society serves as a central source of leadership for the Istanbul Jewish community. The Chief Rabbi and other rabbis are members of the Society, as are almost all the members of the Conseil Laique. In fact, the organization really decides the lists of candidates for election in most organizations, and then its members exercise their voting rights to a much larger extent than the rest of the community, thus ensuring its candidates' election. The men who belong to the Society are well-to-do, well-educated, and are chosen for their leadership potential and interest and their influence in either the Jewish or Turkish communities, or both. The Society has both male and female membership.

In the Conseil Laique, seven members are appointed by the various synagogue councils. One person rarely serves as chairman of the lay council and a synagogue council simultaneously, since it is considered better to have separate individuals as chairmen of the two groups, both for the purpose of soliciting funds and so as not to make leadership too much of a strain upon the individual.

Elections are held for the synagogue councils vaadot kehilla and perhaps for the General Communal Council Vaad Hakelali as well. The size of the councils depends on the size of the synagogue

166

membership. Elections are also held for the boards of directors of the various communal institutions. Usually elections are very poorly attended and the slate is accepted pro forma. In the combined council of Şişli, Beyoglu, and Kasimpassa, it is estimated that only fifty out of ten thousand voters turn out for elections. Recently, however, a new Turkish law concerning organizational elections went into effect, and this might force an improvement in voting participation.

Professional communal leaders include the Chief Rabbi and his staff, as well as directors of the various institutions and their staffs. The Chief Rabbi, David Asseo, is Turkish-born and received his rabbinical ordination in Rhodes. He is also a university graduate. Although observant himself, he is liberal in his approach to religion, permitting worshippers to ride to synagogue and allowing the use of microphones for the services. There are three young rabbis working under him in Istanbul: Eliahu Cohen, Yitzhak Halbe and Moshe Benvenisti, all of whom studied at yeshivot in Israel.

It is understood that the leaders and supporters of Machazike Torah are not in agreement with the activities and attitudes of the other community leaders and have a different set of priorities for the Jewish community.

The Turkish Jewish Community's Relations
with Israel and Diaspora

Turkey has been the only Moslem country to have open diplomatic, commercial and cultural relations with Israel. However, it is in a precarious position

167

because of its connections with the Arab countries, the pro-Moslem interests of many of its citizens, and its own policies toward secularization and Turkish nationalism.

Turkish citizens, as mentioned, are not permitted any formal financial or organization ties with other countries or international organizations. Thus, all Zionist activity and fund-raising for Israel is officially banned. On the other hand, Turkey does permit certain ties on an informal basis. Evidently, the Jewish community is quite afraid of such ties being revealed. For instance when the community was approached in 1972 to contribute to a Torah scroll being contributed by Jewish children around the world to President Shazar, the Chief Rabbi first denied permission for participation and then consented, with the provision that no certificates of contribution be sent, as he was afraid of house searches.

Turkish citizens cannot participate in international Jewish organizations such as the World Jewish Congress or the World Zionist Organization; however, they sometimes attend international conferences as non-listed observers. Even this is done sparingly. The World Jewish Congress was asked to convene a seminar for Community Center and Youth Club heads in Paris, because a number of leaders hesitated about participation in such a seminar in Israel, even as observers, but felt free to go to France. In 1973, however, the seminar was held in Israel.[96] The Chief Rabbi is allowed to attend the International Rabbinical Convention in Israel, just as his Catholic counterpart is allowed to travel to Rome. Similarly, Sephardic Chief Rabbi Nissim of Israel paid an official visit to the Turkish Jewish community in 1966.[97]

It is interesting to note that the Turkish Chief Rabbi handles conversions of Indian women married to B'nai Israel men immigrating to Israel. The Jewish

Agency representative in India is authorized by the Israeli Chief Rabbinate to give courses in Judaism to non-Jewish women married to Jewish men. Upon completion of the course, he sends the women to Istanbul for conversion and then on to Israel.[98]

Many immigrants from Turkey to Israel have returned to Turkey, where it is much easier to maintain a relatively high standard of living. Their return, as well as the prohibition against taking money out of Turkey, has discouraged many more from making the move. The number of Turkish students studying in Israel has also decreased recently. In some cases, parents have refused to finance their children's education if they intended to study in Israel. But because of previous large-scale immigration, most Turkish Jews have relatives in Israel and do travel to Israel for vacations. Almost all of the youth have been to Israel.

Summary

Most of those who know the Jewish community in Turkey believe that it faces extinction. As is the case with most Jewish communities today, its religious life is diminishing and the level of Jewish education among its youth is declining, while inter-marriage and assimilation are increasing. Those Jews who remain in Turkey seem to be more or less content to compromise Jewish identity--if not their own, then that of the coming generations--for economic security and comfort. Even so, they do not feel secure. While the Turkish government is not necessarily hostile to the Jews, its entire orientation combines to make their position tenuous, especially to the extent that they wish to preserve organized Jewish life. The attendant compromises--both those required by the authorities and those which the Jews make voluntarily to be less conspicuous--combine to weaken the fabric of Jewish life.

NOTES

Research Resources

This report is based primarily on available published materials dealing with the post-war Yugoslav
Jewish community, supplemented by personal impressions
gained during a seven-month stay in Yugoslavia in
1971, while doing research for a doctoral dissertation
entitled, "Belgrade, Zagreb, Sarajevo: A Study of
Jewish Communities in Yugoslavia before World War II,"
(Columbia University, 1973). The main sources used
were the publications of the Federation of Jewish
Communities, in particular the following: David Levi-
Dale, ed., Spomenica Savez Jevrejskih opština Jugos-
lavije, 1919-1969 (Commemorative volume on the
fiftieth anniversary of the Federation of Jewish
Communities of Yugoslavia, Belgrade, 1969); Bilten
(Bulletin), 1952-1958; Jevrejski pregled, (Jewish
Review), 1959-1973; and the eight volumes of
Jevrejski almanah from 1954 to 1970. For demographic
data, the most important post-war studies are: Maks
Vajs, "Brethedni rezultati popisa devreja u
Jugoslaviji" (Preliminary Results of the Census of
Jews In Yugoslavia), Jevrejski almanah, 1957-1958, pp.
162-166 and David Perera, "Neki statistički podaci e
Jevrejime u Jugoslaviji u periodu od 1938 do 1965"
(Some statistical data on Jews in Yugoslavia in the
period from 1938 to 1965), ibid., 1968-1970, pp. 135-
147. Of particular value were the results of the 1971
demographic survey published in the following articles
by Marko Peric: "Prvi rezultati našeg demografskog
istraživanja" (First Results of Our Demographic
Survey), Jevrejski pregled, XXIII, Nos. 11-12,
November-December 1972, pp. 2-7; "Dalnji rezultati
našeg demografskog istraživanja" (Further Results...),
ibid., XXIV, Nos. 1-2, January-February, 1973,

pp. 16-21; ibid., Nos. 3-4, March-April, 1973, pp. 31-34; ibid., XXIV, Nos. 5-6, May-June 1973, pp. 2-7; ibid., Nos. 7-8, July-August 1973, pp. 3-6; and "Demographic Study of the Jewish Community in Yugoslavia, 1971-72," Papers in Jewish Demography 1973 (Jerusalem: Institute of Contemporary Jewry, 1977), pp. 267-287. Other noteworthy articles include: Dr. Albert Vajs, "Jevreji u novoj Jugoslaviji" (Jews in the New Yugoslavia), Jevrejski almanah, 1954, pp. 5-47; Dr. Albert Vajs, "Na kraju prve i na početku druge decenije" (At the end of the first and the beginning of the second decade), Jevrejski almanah, 1955-1956, pp. 6-16; and Dr. Lavoslav Kadelburg, "Položaj i perspektive jevrejske zajednice u Jugoslaviji" (The position and perspective of the Jewish community in Yugoslavia), Jevrejski almanah, 1968-1970, pp. 9-17.

Other outside sources consulted include the following: Cvi Rotem, "Yugoslavia--Contemporary Period," Encyclopedia Judaica (N.S.), XVI, pp. 881-885; "Yugoslavia" in Institute of Jewish Affairs of the World Jewish Congress, European Jewry Ten Years After the War (New York, 1956), pp. 180-191; Miriam Steiner, "Yugoslav Jewry," Unity and Dispersion, pp. 223-235 (also in Hebrew in B'tfuzot Hagola, XII, 58/59, Nos. 3/4, 1971-72, pp. 142-153); Cvi Rotem, "The Jews of Yugoslavia in Our Day" (in Hebrew), Gesher, X, No. 3, September 1964, pp. 45-49; and the American Jewish Year Book.

NOTES

The Jewish Community of Yugoslavia

1. David Levi-Dale, ed., Spomenica Saveza jevrejskih opština Juroslavije (Belgrade, 1969), p. 208.

2. "Statistika Jevrejstva Kraljevine Srba, Hrvata i Slovenaca," Jevrejski almanah (O.S.), 1929-30, p. 225. For further information on Yugoslav Jewry prior to World War II, see Harriet Pass Friedenreich, The Jews of Yugoslavia (Philadelphia: Jewish Publication Society, 1979).

3. Saves jevrejskih veroispovednih opština, Izveštaj Glavnog odbera VII kongresu 23 i 24 aprila 1939 godine (Belgrade: Štamparija Beletra, 1939), Table I, p. 82.

4. David Perera, "Neki statistički podaci o Jevrejima u Jugoslaviji u periodu od 1938 do 1965 godine," Jevrejski almanah (N.S.), 1969-70, pp. 140-141.

5. Ibid., p. 142; Spomenica SJOJ, pp. 144-146; Joseph Gordon, "Yugoslavia," American Jewish Yearbook, Vol. 51 (1950), pp. 377-378.

6. Perera, p. 140; Spomenica SJOJ, p. 208.

7. Marko Perić, "Demographic Study of the Jewish Community in Yugoslavia, 1971-72," Papers in Jewish Demography 1973 (Jerusalem: Institute of Contemporary Jewry, 1977), p. 277.

173

8. The preliminary results of this study, organized by city, appeared in a series of articles written by Marko Perić in Jevrejski pregled, 1972-73. The final results for the country as a whole were published in Marko Perić, "Demographic Study of the Jewish Community in Yugoslavia, 1971-1972." All subsequent references to this survey are based on data contained in these articles.

9. Jevrejski pregled, XX, Nos. 7-8, July-August 1969.

10. Zapisnik VIII konferencije Saveze jevrejskih opština Jugoslavije, Belgrade, December 26-27, 1959 (unpublished report, YIVO, New York).

11. Perera, p. 141.

12. Perera, p. 274.

13. Ibid., pp. 270-272 and 284-286.

14. Dr. Albert Vajs, "Jevreji u novoj Jugoslaviji," Jevrejski almanah (N.S.), 1954, p. 43.

15. Spomenica SJOJ, pp. 115-117 and 132-135.

16. Ibid., pp. 183-184; "Jedanaesta konferencija SJOJ," Jevrejski pregled, XXII, Nos. 5-6, May-June 1971, p. 45.

17. Jevrejski pregled, XVII, Nos. 3-4, March-April 1971, p. 45.

18. Spomenica SJOJ, p. 190.

19. SJOJ, Spomenica povodom 50-godišnjica Doma staraca 1910-1960. ed. by David Levi-Dale (Belgrade, 1960).

20. Jevrejski pregled, XXIX, Nos. 3-4, March-April 1971, p. 45.

21. Leon Shapiro, "Yugoslavia," American Jewish Year Book, Vol. 65 (1964), p. 297.

22. Jevrejski pregled, XVI, Nos. 11-12, November-December 1965, p. 31.

23. Ibid., XXI, Nos. 7-8, July-August 1970, pp. 5-8.

24. Ibid., XXII, Nos. 7-8, July-August 1971, p. 16.

25. Ibid., XVII, Nos. 3-4, March-April 1966.

26. Ibid., XIX, Nos. 3-4, March-April 1968, p. 16.

27. Perera, p. 141.

28. Spomenica SJOJ, pp. 122-125.

The Jewish Community of Bulgaria

1. A. Kalev, "Pravnoto Polozhenie Na Evreite v Bulgaria," Novi Dni, Vol. I (IV), 1946, pp. 5-10.

2. Encylopedia of the Jewish Diaspora, Vol. X (Bulgaria), pp. 790-800.

3. Ibid., pp. 824-830.

4. Ibid., p. 898.

5. Ibid., p. 926.

6. Derzhaven Vestnik (Bulgaria), October 16, 1944.

7. JTA, November 22, 1946.

8. Evreisky Vesty, May 12, 1946.

9. Chaim Keshales, History of the Bulgarian Jews, Vol. IV, pp. 18-20.

10. Evreisky Vesty, October 30, 1944.

11. Ibid.

12. A circular of the Jewish Central Committee of the Fatherland Front to all provincial Jewish Fatherland Front Committees, Evreisky Vesty, December 14, 1944.

13. Evreisky Vesty, April 30, 1946.

14. Circular #7 of the United Zionist Organization of April 6, 1946, signed by V. Chaimov.

15. Letter of the United Zionist Organization to the Central Jewish Committee of the Fatherland Front,

May 2, 1946, signed by V. Chaimov. (The letter is in possession of the author.)

16. Concluding protocol of the negotiations between the United Zionist Organization and the Jewish CC of the Fatherland Front, May 15, 1946 (in possession of the author).

17. Poalei Zion, December 5, 1946.

18. Report of the Bulgarian Palestine Committee to the Higher Organization Committee of the United Zionist Organization of May 2 and 3, 1947 (in possession of the author).

19. Interview with Mr. B. Arditi.

20. Evreisky Vesty, October 12, 1946, which reported the meeting, did not specify the date.

21. The author is in possession of a letter of the Women's Zionist Organization of Bulgaria to the Women's Organization of the Fatherland Front, November 22, 1947.

22. Evreisky Vesty, January 18, 1948.

23. Interview with B. Arditi.

24. Evreisky Vesty, March 14, 1948.

25. Evreisky Vesty, March 28, 1948.

26. JTA, October 13, 1946.

27. Evreisky Vesty, October 6, 1946.

28. According to the archives of Mr. M. Levy.

29. Tel-Aviv, WKU/66/9.7/1330--a cablegram signed by the Foreign Minister, M. Chertok.

30. Evreisky Vesty, August 29, 1948.

31. Interview with Mr. Chaim Keshales.

32. Ch. Keshales, op. cit., p. 296.

33. Evreisky Vesty, March 13, 1973.

34. Evreisky Vesty, April 20, 1946.

35. Evreisky Vesty, March 16, 1964.

36. Evreisky Vesty, November 25, 1968.

37. Interview with J.B. (chairman of the Organization's branch in a Bulgarian city in the mid-1960's).

38. Interview with A. Gershon.

39. Evreisky Vesty, November 24, 1961.

40. Evreisky Vesty, November 23, 1970.

41. Evreisky Vesty, February 13, 1967.

42. Evreisky Vesty, November 23, 1970.

43. Ibid.

44. Evreisky Vesty, December 14, 1944.

45. Evreisky Vesty, April 4, 1952.

46. Evreisky Vesty, January 6, 1953.

47. Ibid.

48. _Evreisky Vesty_, December 15, 1957.

49. _Evreisky Vesty_, February 13, 1962.

50. _Evreisky Vesty_, March 22, 1963.

51. Interview with A. Gershon.

52. _Evreisky Vesty_, June 10, 1967.

53. _Evreisky Vesty_, May 27, 1958.

54. S. Israel, "Bulgarian Jews in the Years of People's Regime," in _Godishnik_--1971, p. 128.

55. _Ibid._

56. _Evreisky Vesty_, June 11, 1949.

57. Resolution of the December 1951 plenum of the Central Consistory, _Evreisky Vesty_, February 1, 1952.

58. _Evreisky Vesty_, June 3, 1952.

59. _Ibid._

60. _Evreisky Vesty_, April 28, 1959.

61. _Evreisky Vesty_, April 27, 1962.

62. _Ibid._

63. _Ibid._

64. _Evreisky Vesty_, February 13, 1967.

65. S. Israel, _op_. _cit_., p. 131.

66. _Evreisky Vesty_, March 13, 1972.

67. Evreisky Vesty, February 13, 1967.

68. Evreisky Vesty, March 13, 1972.

69. TASS 10/10, 13.03--"Condemnation of Israel's Aggression" transmitted the statement of the Bulgarian government. Eight minutes later--TASS 10/10, 13.11 the subsequent condemnation of the Organization was transmitted.

The Jewish Community of Greece

1. "The Jewish Community of Greece," Encyclopedia Judaica, 1971, Volume 7, p. 875.

2. Ibid., p. 877.

3. Zvi Bior, Bitfutzot Hagola, Jewish Agency, Winter 1964, p. 256.

4. Encyclopedia Judaica, op. cit., p. 879.

5. Ibid.

6. World Zionist Organization archives, letter, 4/1/78.

7. Joshua Plaut, "The Plight of the Small Jewish Communities in Greece in the aftermath of World War II," Unpublished paper, 1977.

8. Rachel Raphael and Rika Benveniste, private interview, June 25, 1979.

9. Encyclopedia Judaica, op. cit., p. 880; Maurice Goldbloom, "The Community of Greece," American Jewish Year Book, JPS, 1956, Volume 57, p. 362.

10. Menachem Tuano, private interview, August 17, 1972.

11. Goldbloom, op. cit., p. 364.

12. Ibid.

13. Raphael and Benveniste interview.

14. Raphael and Benveniste interview.

15. Plaut, op. cit.

16. Raphael and Benveniste interview; Tuano interview; Plaut, op. cit.

17. Tuano interview.

18. Raphael and Benveniste interview.

19. Victor Semah, American Jewish Year Book, JPS, 1965, Volume 66, pp. 402-403.

20. Steven Bowman, "Remnants and Memories in Greece," Forum, 25, (1976), p. 63.

21. Raphael and Benveniste interview.

22. WZO archives, meeting, 4/1/78.

23. Bowman, op. cit., p. 63.

24. Moshe Keren, private interview, August 16, 1972.

25. Yeshayahu Haran, private interview, August 15, 1972; Keren and Tuano interviews.

26. Yigal Halamit, private interview, September 11, 1979.

27. Goldbloom, op. cit., p. 364.

28. Raphael and Benveniste interview.

29. Sam Modiano, "Greek Jewry's Sunset?," in The Jewish Chronicle, November 26, 1971, p. 80.

30. Haran interview; Modiano, op. cit.

31. Raphael and Benveniste interview.

32. WZO archives, letter, 9/2/78.

33. WZO archives, letter 21/1/79.

34. Haran interview.

35. Modiano, American Jewish Year Book, JPS, 1953, Volume 54, p. 298.

36. Semah, op. cit., p. 403.

37. WZO archives, letter, 26/10/77.

38. The Saga of a Movement, WIZO, 1920-1970, 1970, pp. 81-82.

39. Tuano interview.

40. Modiano, American Jewish Year Book, op. cit., pp. 296-297.

41. Bowman, op. cit., pp. 65, 68.

42. Modiano, American Jewish Year Book, op. cit., pp. 296-297.

43. Plaut, op. cit.

44. Bowman, op. cit., pp. 67-78.

45. Plaut, op. cit.

46. Tuano, Haran interviews.

47. Raphael and Benveniste interview.

48. Tuano interview.

49. Baruch Schreitman, private interview, August 19, 1972.

50. Tuano interview.

51. Mrs. E. Benveniste, letter to Center for Jewish Community Studies, August 25, 1979.

52. Halamit interview.

53. Raphael and Benveniste interview.

54. Bowman, op. cit., pp. 65-67.

55. Ibid, p.70.

56. Bior, Zvi, op. cit., pp. 257-258.

57. Bior, Zvi, Bitfutzot Hagola, Spring, 1962, p. 140.

58. Bowman, op. cit., pp. 65, 67; WZO archives, letter, 7/3/78.

59. New Generation, Pan-Hellenic Jewish Youth Movement, Athens, April 1977.

60. Tuano, Raphael and Benveniste interviews.

61. Raphael and Benveniste interview, Keren interview.

62. WZO archives, letter, 9/11/77.

63. Keren interview.

64. Keren interview.

65. Benveniste letter, op. cit.

66. Bior, _Bitfutzot Hagola_, Winter, 1964, _op. cit._, pp. 257-258.

67. "The Alliance Israelite Universelle," _Encyclopedia Judaica_, Volume 2, p. 651.

68. _Encyclopedia Judaica_, Volume 7, p. 878.

69. WZO archives, letters, 23/6/77; 4/1/78; 7/3/78; Keren interview; Bowman, _op. cit._, pp. 66,67.

70. Andre Deutch, _The Jewish Communities of the World_, WJC, 3rd revised edition, 1971, p. 95.

71. Haran interview.

72. Semah, _op. cit._, p. 364.

73. _Ibid._.

74. Modiano, _American Jewish Year Book_, _op. cit._, p. 298.

75. Semah, _American Jewish Year Book_, JPS, 1960, Volume 61, pp. 220-221.

76. Semah, _American Jewish Year Book_, Volume 66, _op. cit._, p. 404.

77. _Ibid_, p. 401.

78. Modiano, _American Jewish Year Book_, _op. cit._, p. 298.

79. Haran interview.

80. Tuano interview.

The Jewish Community of Turkey

1. Abraham Galante, Histoire des Juifs d'Istanbul, vol. 1, p. 3.

2. Ibid., p. 5.

3. Ibid., p. 7.

4. Ibid., p. 8.

5. Ibid., p. 9.

6. Hayyim Cohen, Hayehudim B'Artzot HaMizrach Hatichon B'Yamenu, p. 17.

7. Ibid.

8. Ibid., p. 18.

9. Ibid., p. 12.

10. Galante, op. cit., pp. 31-32.

11. Cohen, op. cit., pp. 23-24.

12. Galante, op. cit., pp. 32.

13. Cohen, op. cit., p. 25, quoted from Abraham Galante, Turcs et Juifs, pp. 16-22.

14. Cohen, op. cit., p. 77.

15. Ibid, p. 27.

16. Ibid, p. 26.

17. Encyclopedia Judaica, vol. 15, p. 1456.

18. Cohen, op. cit., p. 27.

19. Ibid., p. 27-28.

20. Ibid., p. 28.

21. Galanté, Histoire, p. 45. An editorial published by Dr. Refik Sayadan, President of the Council of Ministers, in the Turkish daily Yeni Sabab interpreted the official Turkish position on Turkish Jewry and Jewish immigration, giving a summary of laws and the government's intentions toward the Jews.

22. Encyclopedia Judaica, Vol. 15, p. 1458.

23. Ibid. Interview of Yisrael Hanukogle.

24. American Jewish Year Book, (AJYB), 1971, Vol. 72, p. 448.

25. American Jewish Year Book, 1967, Vol. 68, p. 417, gives an estimate of 40,000-45,000; Encyclopedia Judaica, Vol. 15, p. 1462, lists the figures at 35,000-40,000.

26. Cohen, op. cit., p. 30.

27. Encyclopedia Judaica, Vol. 15, p. 1462.

28. S. Federbush, World Jewry Today, p. 365.

29. Encyclopedia Judaica, Vol. 15, p. 1462.

30. Cohen, op. cit., p. 29.

31. Ibid.

32. Encyclopedia Judaica, Vol. 15, p. 1462.

33. Cohen, op. cit., p. 78.

34. Ibid.

35. *Ibid.*

36. Interview of Samuel Beezebecher.

37. Interview of Dr. Hayyim Cohen.

38. Cohen, *op. cit.*, p. 76.

39. *Encyclopedia Judaica*, Vol. 15, p. 1460.

40. Andre Deutch, *The Jewish Communities of the World*, 3rd ed., p. 76.

41. *American Jewish Year Book*, Vol. 68, p. 418.

42. Jewish Agency figures.

43. State of Israel, Central Bureau of Statistics, *Special Bulletin* #416.

44. Interview of Mr. Mordechai Mevorah.

45. Interview of Mr. Yisrael Hanukogle.

46. Interview of Mr. Hanukogle.

47. Cohen, *op. cit.*, p. 77.

48. *Ibid.*, p. 96.

49. *Ibid.*

50. *American Jewish Year Book*, Vol. 68, p. 418.

51. Interview of Dr. Cohen.

52. *American Jewish Year Book*, Vol. 68, p. 418.

53. *Ibid.*

54. Ibid.

55. Ibid.

56. Interview of Mr. Hanukogle.

57. Encyclopedia Judaica, Vol. 15, p. 1456.

58. Ibid., p. 1458.

59. American Jewish Year Book, 1962, Vol. 63, p. 396.

60. Ibid.

61. American Jewish Year Book, Vol. 72, p. 448.

62. Interview of Mr. Yeshayahu Haran.

63. American Jewish Year Book, Vol. 72, p. 448; Encyclopedia Judaica, Vol. 15, p. 1463.

64. Interview of Dr. Cohen.

65. Interview of Mr. Hanukogle.

66. American Jewish Year Book, Vol. 63, p. 396.

67. Ibid.

68. Galanté, op. cit., p. 74.

69. Ibid.

70. Ibid.

71. Ibid., p. 98.

72. Ibid., p. 101.

73. *American Jewish Year Book*, Vol. 63, pp. 394-5.

74. *Ibid.*

75. *Ibid.*

76. *American Jewish Year Book*, Vol. 68, p. 419.

77. *Encyclopedia Judaica*, Vol. 15, p. 1460.

78. *American Jewish Year Book*, Vol. 63, p. 395.

79. Cohen, *op. cit.*, p.. 122.

80. *Ibid.*, p. 123.

81. *Ibid.*

82. *American Jewish Year Book*, Vol. 68, p. 418.

83. Deutch, *op. cit.*, p. 77.

84. Cohen, *op. cit.*, p. 29.

85. Interview of Dr. Hayyim Hamiel.

86. Interview of Mr. Hanukogle.

87. *American Jewish Year Book*, Vol. 68, p. 418.

88. Interview of Mr. Yigal Lavi.

89. *Encyclopedia Judaica*, Vol. 15, p. 1462.

90. Interviews of Mr. Lavi, Mr. Mevorah.

91. Interview of Mr. Lavi.

92. Interview of Mr. Hanukogle.

93. Deutch, _op_. _cit_., p. 78.

94. Encyclopedia Judaica, Vol. 15, p. 1462.

95. Interview of Mr. N. Umi-Dvar.

96. The World Zionist Organization, Organization and Information Department, Information Activities January 1973-74 (Report submitted to the Zionist General Council, February 18, 1974).

97. Interview of Mr. Haran.

98. Interview of Professor Daniel J. Elazar.

ABOUT THE AUTHORS

Daniel J. Elazar is overall director of the Study of Jewish Community Organization. Among his various responsibilities, he is President of the Jerusalem Center for Public Affairs, Senator N.M. Paterson Professor of Intergovernmental Relations at Bar-Ilan University, and Senior Fellow of the Center for the Study of Federalism at Temple University. He is the author or editor of numerous books and articles in the field of Jewish political studies, including the recently published Gazetteer of Jewish Political Organization and Kinship and Consent: The Jewish Tradition and its Contemporary Manifestations.

Harriet Pass Friedenreich is an Associate of the Center for Jewish Community Studies and Associate Professor of History at Temple University. She received her Ph.D. in Jewish history at Columbia University and has taught at the University of Judaism. Her study is a product of an extended period of field work in Yugoslavia studying the Jewish communities there from World War I to the present. She is the author of The Jews of Yugoslavia: A Quest for Community, which was published by the Jewish Publication Society in the Center's series on "Jewish Communal and Public Affairs."

Baruch Hazzan was a lecturer in the Political Studies Department of Bar-Ilan University, where he specialized in the politics of Communist Eastern Europe and taught a course on the Jewish communities in those countries. Dr. Hazzan, a native of Bulgaria, has also completed a larger study on the Communist takeover of the Bulgarian Jewish community.

Adina Weiss Liberles was one of the original
research associates of the Center for Jewish Community
Studies, where she was permanently attached to the
Study of Jewish Community Organization. She has an
M.A. in contemporary Jewish studies from Brandeis
University. Among her other contributions to the
worldwide study is a major report on the Jewish
community of Belgium and studies of the Danish,
Finnish, and Swedish Jewish communities.